T0285570

Aporophobia

Aporophobia

Why We Reject the Poor
Instead of Helping Them

Adela Cortina

Translated by
Adrian Nathan West

PRINCETON UNIVERSITY PRESS

PRINCETON AND OXFORD

Published by Princeton University Press
41 William Street, Princeton, New Jersey 08540
99 Banbury Road, Oxford OX2 6JX

press.princeton.edu

Library of Congress Cataloging-in-Publication Data

Names: Cortina Orts, Adela, author.
Title: Aporophobia : why we reject the poor instead of helping
    them / Adela Cortina ; translated by Adrian Nathan West.
Other titles: Aporofobia, el rechazo al pobre. English
Description: Princeton : Princeton University Press, [2022] |
    Includes bibliographical references and index.
Identifiers: LCCN 2021050363 (print) | LCCN 2021050364 (ebook) |
    ISBN 9780691205526 (hardback ; alk. paper) |
    ISBN 9780691239422 (ebook)
Subjects: LCSH: Poor—Moral and ethical aspects. |
    Poverty—Moral and ethical aspects. | Discrimination.
Classification: LCC HC79.P6 C66413 2022 (print) |
    LCC HC79.P6 (ebook) | DDC 362.5—dc23/eng/20211015
LC record available at https://lccn.loc.gov/2021050363
LC ebook record available at https://lccn.loc.gov/2021050364

British Library Cataloging-in-Publication Data is available

Editorial: Hannah Paul and Josh Drake
Production Editorial: Ellen Foos
Text and Jacket Design: Karl Spurzem
Production: Erin Suydam
Publicity: Kate Hensley and Kate Farquhar-Thomson
Copyeditor: Dana Henricks

This book has been composed in Arno Pro with Rustica

Printed on acid-free paper. ∞

Printed in the United States of America

10 9 8 7 6 5 4 3 2 1

Contents

Preface to the English Edition

In August of 2021, there was a drastic earthquake in Haiti, 7.2 on the Richter scale, which led to many dead and wounded and irreparable damage to the country's basic infrastructure. Haiti was already one of the poorest countries in the world, and an inevitable wave of immigration followed. They joined the immense number of Mexicans, Guatemalans, Hondurans, Nicaraguans, and Salvadoreans who had undertaken the harsh journey to the promised land, maybe not a land of milk and honey, but a place where a dignified life was possible.

These people had a well-founded belief that they would find asylum in the promised land, because the triumph of Joe Biden in the recent presidential elections made it appear less likely that the borders would be closed to poor immigrants. A Democrat was back in the White House, open, tolerant, ready to change the course of the country and lead with values shared all across the Western world. The Donald Trump era was over, at least for now: an era when votes were garnered with the promise of building a wall on the Mexican border to keep anyone from crossing via the Rio Grande.

Yes, there was hope. But it was frustrated, because the hostility shown to the Haitians was so ferocious. Many Democrats raised their voices in indignation at the acts of Border Patrol agents who chased immigrants down on horseback. The images on TV, in the papers, and on social media were terrifying.

Once again, we were faced with repression employed against defenseless foreigners only hoping to survive. It seemed that Lady Liberty didn't accept all the tired, the poor, and the hungry equally.

But this isn't just America. Sadly, every country does it, with more or less open displays of aggression. Despite the fundamental role of the Universal Declaration of Human Rights in the EU's identity, Europe has been incapable of developing a plan for taking in those who flee hunger, war, and poverty, crossing the Mediterranean on rafts and arriving at our shores. The Mediterranean, which the Romans called "*mare nostrum*," is now a grave for thousands who had hoped for a better life.

The media and academic texts often describe the rejection of immigrants as xenophobia, fear (*phobia*) of the stranger or foreigner (*xenos*), of those who aren't "one of us." It's true that there is a tendency to shut the door to strangers, so deeply rooted that some writers affirm that the human brain itself is xenophobic. We will look at that later, but for now I would like to ask a simple question that gets at the very point of this book: Do we reject immigrants because they are foreign or because they are poor and seem to bring problems while offering nothing of value in return?

It doesn't seem hard to answer. No one is bothered by the foreigners who flock to Vegas to spend money in casinos or Chinese billionaires investing their money in safe havens; nobody's bothered by foreign scientists or professors, who are often hired with handsome salaries. Foreign elite athletes, artists, and chefs get the royal treatment, no matter where they come from. And everywhere people are happy to show hospitality to foreign tourists, who contribute a great deal to many countries' GDP. One of the worst consequences of the COVID-19 pandemic has been the drastic reduction of international travel, which has been a catastrophe for restaurants and other tourism-dependent sectors.

In regards to the aforementioned cases, not only does "xenophobia" not apply, we can even talk of "xenophilia," of friendship toward the foreigner. *Toward a certain type of foreigner.* This is quite a different feeling from that aroused by poor foreigners, whom we reject not because of their origin, but because of their status. Their race or ethnic group isn't the problem: the problem is they come here to complicate the lives of people who feel the need to defend what they have against those who seem to have nothing but problems to contribute.

We tell all kinds of nasty stories about these people: they take our jobs, they're terrorists or criminals, their values are antidemocratic. They're a threat to well-being in our societies, where there may be poverty and inequality, it's true, but nothing that can be compared to the wars, the misery, and the tyranny across our borders.

The sentiment behind these stories is *aporophobia*, not xenophobia: fear of and contempt for the poor (*aporos*), the defenseless person who appears to have nothing to give. It's a problem for the poor foreigner, but also for the poor native, the person we've lived with as long as we can remember. An example in my native Spain, as in many other countries, is the *gitanos* (Romani people), who often live on the margins and are the object of wariness and suspicion unless they're famous Flamenco stars. And yet these people are no less "native" to their countries than anyone else. The same is true of Native Americans, of African Americans, of the indigenous peoples of Latin America, and an endless number of so-called minorities (who are often the numerical majority) in countries all over the world.

I am not denying the existence of xenophobia and racism. They're real, and there are mountains of research that attest to it. Misogyny, antisemitism, christianophobia, islamophobia, homophobia, and transphobia are all realities. Some may say we talk about them too much, but these are social pathologies and they need to be diagnosed and treated. Ending these phobias is a matter of respect, not respect for "human dignity," which is an abstraction without a face, but for concrete individuals who have dignity and not just a price.

What interests us about aporophobia in this book is the way it cuts across these other prejudices, often lies at their root, and is excluded from the social contract and the principles of generosity that necessarily underlie it. The idea of *homo economicus*, rationally pursuing his individual interests, has been overemphasized with respect to that of *homo reciprocans*, who gives not necessarily for direct benefit, but for the betterment of a community, which also redounds to him.

It has now been fifty years since John Rawls published *A Theory of Justice*, which recovered the contractual tradition as an instrument for liberal democratic societies to better understand themselves. Contractual societies are an advance over the state of nature, in which conflicts are resolved through violence. But the principle of exchange has limits, too, when interpreted in such a way that society only permits entry to those who can offer it something in return.

Rawls avoids this limit because the hypothetical contract his work speaks of aims not at the formation of a political community, but at the selection of principles of justice that liberal democratic societies must heed, and one of these is difference, specifically the difference of the less advantaged. Unfortunately, there is an immense difference in contractual societies between *what ought to be* and *what is*.

Anytime an offer is made, implicitly or explicitly, people ask themselves, "What do I get out of it?" We are beings with inadequacies and needs and we address them with education, but also with what others can give us. This is the basis of the rule of law, which guarantees us protection if we fulfill our duties and responsibilities. And this in turn gives rise to the major institutions of the political, economic, and cultural world, which promise to defend the ever-vulnerable citizenry. The poor seem to break with this game of quid pro quo: our minds, inclined to calculations, sense that they can only bring problems, and so the tendency to exclude them prevails.

This book is about the undeniable, everyday reality of aporophobia, the need to put a name to it in order to recognize it and to look for causes and propose ways of overcoming it. This is important because aporophobia is a ubiquitous and almost invisible affront to the dignity, welfare, and happiness of the people who are its victims. Further, it is an attitude universal in scope: every human being harbors aporophobia, and there are neurological and social reasons for this that can be and should be modified if we intend to take seriously at least two key elements of our culture: respect for the equal dignity of all persons and compassion—understood as the capacity to perceive the suffering of others and the commitment to ameliorate it. Finally, aporophobia represents a challenge to democracy. And democracy is getting weaker all the time. Research shows that since the nineties, it has entered into a process of deconsolidation at the same time as autocracy has risen. To all appearances, the fears stoked by the pandemic have only worsened this, convincing many people that security and prosperity are preferable to freedom, with some alleging that China's authoritarian model has done a better job of preserving the lives and well-being of its citizenry than democratic countries.

Democratic societies have ignored their social dimensions for too long—that sphere of rights related to cultural and economic claims that should form the nucleus of contemporary democracies. This lacuna affects the poor above all, and for that reason, aporophobia is also a threat to democracy.

As always, a book owes a debt to the many people who, consciously or unconsciously, assisted in its creation. Their names will appear throughout these pages, but I would like to mention something about the tradition I am working within, the Kantian one, but with two particular strands: first, the discourse ethics that Karl-Otto Apel and Jürgen Habermas formulated in the 1970s, and second, John Rawls and those who have followed him, including Amartya Sen, Martha Nussbaum, David Crocker, Georges Enderle, Flavio Comim, and Gustavo Pereira. Also important for my work have been authors in a parallel field, that of human development ethics, in particular Denis Goulet.

Some of these thinkers are, like myself, members of IDEA, the *International Development Ethics Association*. Dialoguing and debating with them has been a gift, and I will always be grateful to them for it.

Finally, I also owe a debt in this book to my work group, which brings together professors and researchers from the Universities of Valencia, Castellón, and Murcia and Valencia's Polytechnic University. To Jesús Conill, Domingo García-Marzá, Salvador Cabedo, Juan Carlos Siurana, Elsa González, Emilio Martínez, José Félix Lozano, Agustín Domingo, Pedro Jesús Pérez Zafrilla, Javier Gracia, Pedro Jesús Teruel, Ramón Feenstra, Patrici Calvo, César Ortega, Andrés Richart, Martha Rodríguez, and Marina García Granero. My continuous debates, discussions, and dialogues with them about these subjects are the soil out of which this book has grown.

In addition, our group's work has been made possible under the aegis of the Projects in Scientific Investigation and Technological Development Frameworks FFI2013-47136-C2-1-P and

FFI2016-76753-C2-1-P, financed by the Ministry of the Economy and Competitivity, and under the purview of the excellence research group of the Generalitat Valenciana PROMETEO 2009/085.

My thanks to all of them.

Valencia, October 2021

Introduction

In the course of 2016, more than seventy-five million tourists entered Spain from abroad. Beyond the usual reasons for coming to the country, there were major problems in many other vacation destinations, leading to a significant increase in the already massive number of visitors. The media reported the news with an enthusiasm bordering on euphoria, breaking down the figures from month to month, and the audience tuned in with equal enthusiasm, because for some time now, tourism has been Spain's main source of income, particularly since the explosion of the real estate bubble and the disastrous economic, financial, and political crisis that followed it. Creating jobs that might slowly become less precarious, raising the occupancy rates of hotels with all that means for bars, restaurants, and shops—this is one of the promises tourism always brings.

These tourists come from other countries: excellent. Sometimes they belong to other ethnic groups and other races—I say this in full awareness of the difficulties involved in clarifying what ethnic groups and races even are. If we had to choose an adjective to describe them in Spanish, it would be *extranjero*— "foreigner," or *xenos* in Greek. The latter word we know well, unfortunately, as the root of the term *xenophobia*, which means "rejection, fear, or hostility toward the foreign, that which comes from elsewhere, the person who isn't one of us, the stranger."

This brings us to a question that, curiously, no one asks: When they come to our country, do these foreign tourists awaken a feeling of xenophobia—this sadly still-relevant expression—among the Spanish population? Do these foreigners feel rejected, do they give rise to that fear or aversion that are the meaning of the Greek *phobos*?

Rarely has a question been easier to answer: no, they do not inspire rejection in the least. To the contrary, people bend over backwards to attend to them at hotels, in stores, in apartments, on the beach, at rental villas in the country. Not only do they tell them the best route in detail when they ask for directions— they even accompany them to the place in question. They'll do anything to cater to tourists' whims, to make them feel at home or better than at home. What everyone wants most is for them to come back.

And so it is impossible to speak here of xenophobia, however much we hear this term bandied about in conversation or in the media. We'd do better to speak of *xenophilia*, love and friendship for the foreigner. *For this particular type of foreigner.*

Of course all this could be the product of a basic sense of hospitality toward whomever comes from elsewhere, a natural desire to share the beaches, the good climate, and our artistic heritage. After all, we have been cultivating this tradition of hospitality in the East and West since ancient times, especially in the countries of southern Europe.

And yet, if we really think about it, taking into consideration the cases of other people who came to Spain from elsewhere in 2016 and even before, we will have to admit, much to our regret, that this attitude of embracing the foreigner cannot be as deeply rooted as we think. I am referring to people who came from the *other* side of the Mediterranean and risked and often

lost their lives to reach the supposed promised land of the
European Union.

These aren't tourists leaving behind a trail of money in
greater or lesser quantities, depending on their resources or
their largesse. They are political refugees and poor immigrants.
They are a different kind of foreigner. Their exodus has its begin-
nings far away in space and time. They haven't come to our
country for the sun, the beaches, or the natural and artistic
beauty, let alone for our proverbial hospitality, which doesn't
apply to them. They have been torn from their homes by war,
hunger, and misery; they have placed themselves in the hands
of exploitative mafias, they have set off on rafts and in lifeboats,
and they are trying any way they can to reach our coasts. Thousands of them die at sea, and the ordeal continues for them in
inhospitable countries with resentful populations, in despicable
internment camps, with the risk of being sent back always present. Their sole, scant consolation is that they need not yearn for
the pots of meat in Egypt, the way the Israelites did in Exodus.

As we know, the refugee crisis has been growing in Europe
since 2007, and it reached a flashpoint in 2011 with the beginning
of the war in Syria; millions of people have been fleeing from conflict zones since 2001. Nonetheless, since 2015, the migrant crisis
in Europe has been the largest since the Second World War. Its
victims are desperate people fleeing from Syria, Lebanon, Afghanistan, Eritrea, Nigeria, Albania, Pakistan, Iraq, Sudan, Gambia,
and Bangladesh, the majority of them crossing through Greece
and Italy. Their stories aren't fiction—they are raw and real.

News media present one account after another, month
after month, year after year, in a spirit of conformism and in the
flat tone used to discuss something inevitable—but this isn't
inevitable.

There's no way to avoid comparing the eager and welcoming attitude toward foreigners who show up as tourists with the merciless rejection of waves of poor immigrants. Doors are closed in their faces, fences and walls are raised, borders closed. Angela Merkel lost votes in her country, even in her own party, for her kindness and persistence in showing a basic degree of humanity; England rejected immigrants and closed ranks, choosing Brexit; the number of voters supporting nationalist parties has risen vertiginously in France, Austria, Germany, Hungary, and the Netherlands; and Donald Trump emerged victorious, among other reasons, thanks to his promise to deport Mexican immigrants and build a wall along the Mexican border. Some of his votes seem to have come from former immigrants now settled in their new homeland.

There isn't a single country where we can speak of xenophilia with regard to the feelings aroused by refugees and poor immigrants. There is no sense of love or friendship for the foreigner. But we can't call this xenophobia either, because what gives rise to this rejection, this aversion, isn't the fact that these people come from elsewhere, that they are from another race or ethnic group—it isn't foreigners as such that are offensive. *What is offensive is that they are poor*, that they are here to complicate things for people trying to defend their way of life, for better or worse—that they bring with them problems, not resources.

The poor people who offend us, the destitute or the homeless, those who can't contribute to their country's GDP or ours, seem to create nothing but difficulties. They include freeloaders who will inflate our health care costs, migrant workers who will take jobs away from citizens, potential terrorists; their values are dubious, and they'll upset the well-being of our societies. Maybe we have poverty and inequality too, but it's nothing like those of people fleeing war and misery.

We can't call this xenophobia. It is rather a clear-cut case of *aporophobia*, of rejection, aversion, fear, and contempt for the poor, for those without resources, who seem incapable of paying us back in any worthwhile way.

Of course, xenophobia and racism exist: distrust of foreigners and people of other races, ethnic groups, or cultures, wariness of whatever is different. There is, alas, much data to prove it, just as there is to prove the reality of misogyny, Christianophobia, Islamophobia, and homophobia. Some people may complain that contemporary society is overly centered on these phobias, but they do exist, they are social pathologies, and we need to diagnose and treat them. Getting rid of them is necessary in order to show respect not to *human dignity*, which is an abstraction without a visible face, but rather concrete people, who are the real possessors of dignity and cannot be reduced to cost/benefit calculations.

And yet, we will not be addressing this sort of rejection in the present book. Instead we will look at an aversion that frequently lies at its root and that goes even further: *aporophobia*, the contempt for the poor, the rejection of the person who takes but cannot give back, or at least seems unable to give back. And who, for that reason, is excluded from the world built on political, economic, and social contracts, a world of giving and receiving, in which only those who seem to have something interesting to offer in return are welcome.

Anytime an offer is made, implicitly or explicitly, people ask themselves, "What do I get out of this?" We are beings with inadequacies and needs and we address them with education, but also with what others can give us. This is the basis of the rule of law, which guarantees us protection if we fulfill our duties and responsibilities. And this in turn gives rise to the major institutions of the political, economic, and cultural world, which promise to defend the ever-vulnerable citizenry. The poor seem to break with this game of quid pro quo: our minds, inclined to calculations, sense that they can only bring problems, and so the tendency to exclude them prevails.

This book is about the undeniable, everyday reality of aporophobia, the need to put a name to it in order to recognize it and to look for causes and propose ways of overcoming it. This is important because aporophobia is an ever-present and almost invisible affront to the dignity, welfare, and happiness of the people who are its victims. Further, it is an attitude universal in scope: every human being harbors aporophobia, and there are neurological and social reasons for this that can be and should be modified if we truly intend to take seriously at least two key elements of our culture: respect for the equal dignity of all persons and compassion—understood as the capacity to perceive the suffering of others, and the commitment to trying to avoid it.

As always, a book owes a debt to the many people who, consciously or unconsciously, assisted in its creation. Their names will appear throughout these pages, but I would prefer to thank from the outset Emilio Martínez Navarro, who has been dealing with the challenge of aporophobia since it first arose, in theory as well as in practice. And my work group, which brings together professors and researchers from the Universities of Valencia, Castellón, and Murcia and Valencia's Polytechnic University. To Jesús Conill, Domingo García-Marzá, Salvador Cabedo, Juan Carlos Siurana, Elsa González, José Félix Lozano, Agustín Domingo, Francisco Arenas, Sonia Reverter, Pedro Jesús Pérez Zafrilla, Javier Gracia, Pedro Jesús Teruel, Ramón Feenstra, Patrici Calvo, Lidia de Tienda, Daniel Pallarés, Joaquín Gil, César Ortega, Andrés Richart, and Marina García Granero.

My continuous debates, discussions, and dialogues with them about these subjects are the soil out of which this book has grown.

In addition, our group's work has been made possible under the aegis of the Projects in Scientific Investigation and Technological Development Frameworks FFI2013-47136-C2-1-P and FFI2016-76753-C2-1-P, financed by the Ministry of the Economy and Competitiveness, and under the purview of the excellence research group of the Generalitat Valenciana PROMETEO 2009/085. The University of Valencia likewise aided me greatly with a sabbatical semester during the 2015–2016 academic year in order to write this book.

My thanks to all of them.

Valencia, January 2017

Chapter 1

A Scourge without a Name

Many years later as he faced the firing squad, Colonel Aureliano Buendía was to remember that distant afternoon when his father took him to discover ice. At that time Macondo was a village of twenty adobe houses, built on the bank of a river of clear water that ran along a bed of polished stones, which were white and enormous, like prehistoric eggs. The world was so recent that many things lacked names, and in order to indicate them it was necessary to point.[1]

From Xenophobia to Aporophobia

At the beginning of his extraordinary novel *One Hundred Years of Solitude*, Gabriel García Márquez recreates the setting of the book of Genesis, but situated in Macondo, the Colombian village where the saga of the Buendía family takes place, rather than in the Garden of Eden between the Tigris and Euphrates Rivers. His text, like the biblical one, states that at the beginning of time, many things lacked a name and had to be pointed out with the finger.

Human history, at least to an extent, consists of naming things in order to incorporate them into the human world through dialogue, consciousness, and reflection, through words and writing, without which those things cannot become a part of us. The adobe houses and the polished stones of the river can be pointed out, but how do we describe personal and social realities in order to recognize them when they lack a physical form?

It's impossible to point a finger at democracy, freedom, conscience, totalitarianism, beauty, hospitality, or finance capitalism; it's impossible to physically indicate xenophobia, racism, misogyny, homophobia, Christianophobia, or Islamophobia. These are social realities that require names which allow us to recognize them and know of their existence—to analyze them and to take a position with respect to them. Otherwise, they linger in the fog of anonymity, where they may act as an ideology in a sense similar to the one Marx intended: as a deformed and deforming vision of reality filtered through the dominant class or dominant groups in a given time and context to maintain their dominant status. The more silent it is, the more effective an ideology is, because it cannot even be denounced. It distorts reality by concealing it, wrapping it in a cloak of invisibility, making it impossible to see its outlines. It is for this reason that history consists in part of naming things, both those we can point out and those we can't, because they form part of the fabric of social reality rather than of the physical world.

This has occurred with xenophobia and racism, which are old as humanity itself, but which can be addressed now that they have been given a name. What is unique about such phobias is that they are founded not in a personal history of hatred toward a given person who has been a source of bad experiences for oneself or for one's ancestors. Instead, it is something stranger. It is a distaste for certain people with whom, most often, one isn't even acquainted, because they bear the characteristics of a group that the person experiencing this phobia considers deserving of fear or contempt, or of both at the same time.

In all cases, the person who feels this contempt adopts an attitude of superiority vis-à-vis the other, considering his own ethnic group, race, sexual tendency, or belief—whether religious or atheistic—to be superior and thus a source of legitimacy for rejecting the other. This is a key point about group-based phobias: the conviction that there exists an asymmetrical relationship, that the race, ethnic group, sexual orientation, religious belief or lack thereof of the person who feels contempt is superior to that of the person being rejected. And this justifies attacking that person physically or with words—which are themselves a mode of action.

In the task of legitimating such doubtful choices, the interpretive capacities of the brain play an important role, the way they work to weave a calming story that allows us to remain in equilibrium. The belief in one's own superiority is one that works well in day-to-day life, even if this presumed superiority has no basis whatsoever in biology or culture.

As we will see in the following chapter, in democratic countries, which declare themselves in favor of the equality and dignity of all human beings, recognizing cases of xenophobia, racism, homophobia, and abuse is a task for the courts and the police—an arduous one, too, not simply because hate crimes or instances of hatred are rarely reported or because there is a lack of resources for dealing with them. It's true that it's extremely difficult to tell when a discourse against a given group may be considered a hate crime of the kind legally proscribed and subject to sanction and when it is falls under the protections accorded to freedom of expression. What makes matters worse is the abundance of political parties that have opted for xenophobic discourses as a mark of identity and an incentive for getting votes. Alas, it has proven a winning strategy, particularly in moments of crisis, when a sacrificial lamb is just the thing for those who have nothing positive to offer.

However old xenophobia and racism are, they were not recognized as such until a certain moment in history, when people finally pointed a finger at them, gave them a name, and analyzed them with reference to the social demand of respect for human dignity. It is impossible to respect people as such and at the same time attack individuals for the mere fact of belonging to a group. We must keep in mind that hateful words are not merely a provocation to the violation of another's dignity—they themselves constitute such a violation.

And yet, although xenophobia is clearly on the rise in the countries of the European Union, particularly since the beginning of the 2008 economic crisis, it isn't clear, if we look at things from a broader perspective, that mere hatred of the other accounts for what is happening.

To take an example already mentioned in the introduction to the present book: on June 25, 2016, no sooner than the results of the Brexit referendum were made known, with a small majority of voters declaring themselves in favor of leaving, the press published stories of interest for residents of Great Britain and Spain. It turned out the British were worried because Spanish immigrants working in the health care sector constituted a large number of the country's doctors and nurses and were, moreover, highly qualified. These were skilled immigrants, highly educated, who contributed to the country's GDP and to improving the well-being of the population.

Naturally, no matter how *foreign* they were, there wasn't the least interest in expelling these people; rather, it was a relief to realize that the process of abandoning the European Union would be long enough that there was no reason to worry about these fine professionals being forced to leave the country. The famous *in-in* and *out-out* was suspended as pragmatisms from both sides of the divide worked slowly through the actual process of separation. The famous affirmation *Brexit is Brexit* was an attractive slogan for a meaningless proposal. No one knows what the real nature of this departure of Britain from the European Union will bring, and no one seems particularly to desire it, not even the many people who voted Leave and then excoriated their politicians for lying to them.

Curiously, at the same time, in Spain we were asking ourselves about the fate of the large number of British immigrants living on the Spanish coasts, especially in the south and east, who bring a great deal of money wherever they reside. These foreigners took advantage of the sun and the national health care system, but Spain also had an interest in keeping them in the country. Here, too, the ambiguity concerning what the Brexit process would actually consist of, and the lack of clarity around the famous Article 50 of the Treaty on the European Union, served as a kind of life preserver.

And so, specialized health care personnel interest the United Kingdom, and British retirees looking to spend their last days in the sun interest Spain. In neither case is there the least sign of aversion. Hence, it is not the foreigner as such that inspires rejection. There may be an uncertainty in given dealings, because language differences and distinct habits make interactions less clear than they are with those who share our language and our traditions, but this is not the same as aversion and rejection.

Nor are we repulsed by people from the East who buy up whole soccer teams or bring what used to be called "petrodollars," or soccer players of whatever ethnic group or race, who make millions and are essential for winning games. We don't mind those Romani people who make their name in the flamenco world, and we don't reject foreign investors who build automobile factories, bars, and clubs in our country. In these and many other ways, foreigners contribute to the growth of the country's GDP.

Our doors close, however, before political refugees, poor immigrants who have nothing to lose but their chains, Romani people selling tissues in rough neighborhoods and digging around in trash containers, when in reality they are no less native to the country than anyone else, however much their culture pertains to a minority. The doors of conscience close before homeless beggars, who are condemned to invisibility worldwide.

And so the problem isn't race, ethnicity, or foreign birth. The problem is poverty. And worst of all, whereas there are many racists and many xenophobic people, almost everyone is aporophobic.

It is the poor person, the *aporos*, who is an irritation, even to his own family. The poor relative is considered a source of shame it is best not to bring to light, while it is a pleasure to boast of a triumphant relation well situated in the academy, politics, art, or business. It is a phobia toward the poor that leads us to reject individuals, races, and ethnic groups that in general lack resources and that therefore cannot—or appear unable to—offer anything.

History of a Term

The conviction that rejection of the poor is more widespread and ingrained than other sorts of aversion, that it is a powerful personal and social reality, as we see constantly in our daily lives, is one I expressed in a column I published decades ago in a newspaper in Spain. José Antonio Marina and I shared a section of *ABC Cultural* entitled Ethical Creation, where once a week we presented articles, book reviews, and columns devoted to ethics in the broad sense of the term, examining not only morals but also the economy and politics. This is how Adam Smith understood it, and as a professor of philosophy he both engaged with the moral sentiments and also sought the sources of wealth and poverty among nations. Politics and economy were essential to our Ethical Creation because without them, the vision of the moral world would remain truncated.

It was on December 1, 1995, that I published a column with the title "Aporophobia." In it, I made reference to a Euro-Mediterranean conference that took place in Europe around that time and attempted to address burning issues in the countries of that region, issues that remain points of contention to this day: immigration, terrorism, and peace processes. Nowadays, we must include among them the economic crisis and unemployment. It was easy to predict that experts all over the world would describe racism, xenophobia, and religious fundamentalism as the greatest problems in the Mediterranean region. But I already sensed—and I continue to feel this way—that the basis of all of those was a rejection, aversion, fear directed toward the poor, one that still didn't have a name.

And a label for this social pathology was urgently needed in order to diagnose it more precisely and propose effective treatments. Doing so would be a fitting objective for Mediterranean culture, which has been accustomed to dialogue since the time of Socrates—accustomed, in other words, to what is by definition an inclusive activity. For the same reason, at the end of the twentieth century, it was imperative that dialogue be the medium of exploration of the necessity of providing the underprivileged with what belongs to them by birth: the enjoyment of a culturally and materially dignified life.

Convinced that we do not so much reject foreigners as the poor, I looked in my Greek dictionary from my student days for a term that designated the poor person, the person lacking in resources, and I found the word *aporos*. I used it to coin the term *aporophobia* by analogy with *xenophobia* and *homophobia*.

A second milestone in the history of this word was a chapter in a textbook put together by a team of professors for the publisher Santillana and published for the first time in 1996. Domingo García-Marzá, María Begoña Domené, Emilio Martínez, Juan Manuel Ros, Norberto Smilg, and I collaborated on it, and the experience was exhilarating. The title was *Ethics: Moral Life and Ethical Reflection*, and it was for a required course for students in their fourth year of secondary school that boasted two virtues very rare in our country: it provoked no objections on the part of any political or social group, and no one demanded it compete with any other subject in the curriculum. If only the situation had continued that way—as a mandatory course in ethics, period—we could have saved ourselves more than a few sterile arguments.

As the title clearly reflects, the book intended to approach its subject matter from two perspectives: that of daily life, in which people follow distinctive patterns of personal conduct dictated by ideals, norms, or conceptions of the life well lived, and that of ethics and moral philosophy, which have contributed to our understanding of duty and led us to search for the bases of norms, ideals, or projects.

In the book's sixth chapter, we discussed a basic challenge to human dignity and democratic life in common, namely the undeniable reality of social and economic discrimination. After explaining that discrimination is a social matter and what exactly it comprises, there was a section entitled "Aporophobia: The Poor and the Disabled Are Pushed Aside." Accompanied by Eduardo Galeano's extraordinary text, *The Nobodies*, it analyzed the vice of aporophobia, and suggested the solution we will attempt to sketch out briefly in this book: the creation of equality through education and institutions.

Later, the text dealt with other forms of social discrimination: racism, homophobia, and prejudice against other, less talked about groups like the old or the physically disabled. The message was clear: a moral and political culture based on the equal dignity of all would need to replace those everyday hatreds.

A third milestone in the present history of the word *aporophobia* was an article I published in *El País* on March 7, 2000. In it, I discuss the Royal Spanish Academy's debate over including the neologism "aporophobia" to its *Dictionary of the Spanish Language*. It offered as a possible definition: "hatred, repugnance, or hostility toward the poor, the underprivileged, or the homeless." And they added, in one of those illuminating parentheses that follow the word, "(From the Greek *aporos*, poor, and *phobos*, fear)."

To my knowledge, this expression doesn't exist in other languages, and I am not sure it is the best term we could contrive. But what cannot be doubted is there is a need to put a name to the rejection of the poor and helpless, because the attitude is only worse to the extent that it is unnamed. Without recognition, this undeniable reality cannot be effectively addressed.

The Royal Academy has strict criteria for introducing new words into its dictionary, which includes expressions from all Spanish-speaking countries. So far as I know, the most common justifications are that the word appears in classic works of the Spanish language or proceeds from a foreign language but has come to be widely used in Spanish. For example, many English terms have been added in recent years. But I believe that beyond that, what matters as much or more is that the term *aporophobia* designates a reality so present in social life that it cannot be fully understood without it. Today, life cannot be understood without naming those phobias that produce rejection of people whose characteristics place them in a group that is despised, feared, or both. One of these is aporophobia, the rejection of the poor.

In my opinion, we need a name not to add a few paragraphs to the dictionary, but to aid us in recognizing this very present, very painful reality, to recognize it, study its causes, and decide whether it can be accepted or whether it is our duty to suppress it. This must be done because rejection of the poor degrades the person who practices it and is a constant assault on the dignity of real people with names. Not against the abstraction of "human dignity," but against the dignity and welfare of flesh-and-blood people who suffer rejection. In this book, we will argue that there is no one who has nothing to offer. Emilio Martínez, author of the entry *Aporophobia* in the *Glossary for an Intercultural Society*, published by the Bancaja Foundation in 2002, says the same.

Finally, we must point out that the term *aporophobia* has aroused the interest of many people committed to empowering the poor. It has served as a rubric for conferences and meetings of civil society organizations; the RAIS Foundation has used it to better explain the violence suffered by the homeless; and it has also figured in recent analyses of integration policies for immigrant communities in Europe, among them the publications of Professor Silveira Gorski. The media have employed it to discuss the abuse of the poor and indigent, and it has been the subject of more than one dissertation. Wikipedia has added the term to its dictionary, and the Spanish Ministry of the Interior uses it to describe crimes committed against the poor.

More significant to me, however, is that when I speak of aporophobia in a conference or workshop on either side of the

Atlantic, my listeners, young and old, smile and nod understandingly, as if to say, "That's true, that's something we see every day."

Ortega y Gasset said that what's happening is that we do not know what's happening, and for this reason, we must become aware of what is happening with us in regard to the constant contempt for the poor. When I see the agreement on the faces of people when I explain what aporophobia is, I realize it is a reality that is very close—all too close—to us.

Socrates's imperative to know oneself initiated the first enlightenment, which took place in Classical Greece. In the same line, the Kantian invitation to employ one's own reason gave rise to the glow of the Enlightenment proper. Knowing more and more about ourselves, recognizing that this form of discrimination we have dubbed *aporophobia* for lack of a better word exists, inquiring as to its causes, and searching for ways to overcoming it, is one of the challenges of our time. The name is a simple path to recognition, because, as an excellent professor of mine, Fernando Cubells, used to say, questions of words are solemn questions of things.

Throughout this book, we will attempt to offer an antidote to this wound, one that will require both formal and informal education and the creation of institutions aimed at overcoming prejudice. The antidote is active respect for the equal dignity of people in daily life, and it demands the cordial recognition of that dignity. This will be the wellspring of compassion, but not just any sort of compassion: rather the kind that Stefan Zweig describes at the beginning of his splendid novel *Beware of Pity* with the following words:

> There are two kinds of compassion. One is faint-hearted and sentimental, it, in essence, is nothing but the impatience of the heart, hurrying to quickly get rid of the painful sensation

at the sight of someone else's misfortune; it is not compassion, but only an instinctive desire to protect your peace from the suffering of your neighbor. But there is another compassion—true, which requires action, not sentimentality, it knows what it wants, and is full of determination, suffering and compassion, to do everything that is human and even beyond them.[2]

Recognition of equal dignity and compassion is the key to an ethics of cordial reason and is indispensable to the overcoming of inhumane discrimination.[3]

Chapter 2

Hate Crimes toward the Poor

The Key to Hatred: The Holder or
the Object of Contempt?

On March 17, 2016, several Spanish newspapers reported on a shameful event that took place in Madrid the day before. A large number of people had gathered in the Plaza Mayor to enjoy a day of sun before a soccer game between Atlético de Madrid and PSV Eindhoven. A group of Romani women were begging in the square when the fans of the Dutch team came along. With an air of disdain, the fans gave the women money, but humiliated them while doing so, throwing coins at them and making them dance and do pushups in exchange for their charity. Journalists described this as an instance of aporophobia, and sought the opinions of various parties, including Emilio Martínez, myself, members of Hatento, which monitors hate crimes against the homeless, and the Fundación Secretariado Gitano. All of us saw the matter as an evident case of discrimination, aporophobia, and *machismo* that infringed upon the right to dignity that every person is entitled to, and each of us had several other observations on the matter.

But the first comments to appear below the article in *El Mundo* were the very opposite of what we had affirmed. One person claimed to have witnessed the events and stated that the women were stealing, not begging, that they were a gang of Romanian "gypsies" who prefer robbing tourists and Spaniards to working. And this person added unambiguously: "This is a blotch on Madrid and gives the city a bad name," before scorning the notion of these women as victims and concluding sarcastically: "At this rate, the government will soon give them all apartments (I'm not kidding)." A second commenter said the fans may have felt aporophobia after seeing reports on the economics of begging or because they were not used to their leisure moments being ruined by noisy accordions and people begging for change. A question seems to impose itself here: what is the cause of phobias, contempt or the object of contempt?

Here it is not especially difficult to respond, because one can refuse to give alms to a beggar for any number of reasons that have nothing to do with rejection or contempt. Perhaps one prefers to contribute to charitable organizations that aid others with a knowledge of the causes of poverty and a sense of justice and oppose the degrading act of seeking charity. Perhaps one prefers to pressure the local government to use public monies to attend to the basic needs of citizens. But what is inadmissible under any circumstances is humiliation, disdain, that miserable sense of superiority that is no more dignified than the status of its victims. The source of hatred and contempt is in the person who feels them, not the person subject to them.

In his book, *The Discourse of Hate,* André Glucksmann argues that hatred exists, that we must overcome our idealism and accept the existence of hatred; and he devotes the three major sections of the text to an analysis of three kinds of hatred that persist in the contemporary world, but the roots of which lie far back in time: anti-Americanism, antisemitism, and misogyny. In all three, according to Glucksmann, the key to hatred resides in the person who hates, not in the collective object of hatred. "They key to antisemitism," he affirms, "is the anti-Semite, not the Jew."[1] We will resort to this insight throughout the present book, because those who evince a phobia inevitably justify it by laying blame on the group they disparage. And in all cases, this is a mere excuse.

Hate Crimes, Hate Speech: Two Social Pathologies

In November of 2015, I received a letter from Luis Carlos Perea, Director of Strategic Development for the RAIS Foundation, in which he remarked that the concept of aporophobia had been useful to the foundation for describing certain kinds of violence, particularly the violence suffered by the homeless. Homelessness is a profound social problem that places a person on the extreme edge of vulnerability. The person who lacks even the protection of a home, however precarious it may be, lacks the minimum of necessary privacy and has virtually no protection against external aggression, degradation, the whims of stupid people who wish to amuse themselves at others' expense or of bitter people wishing to take their rage out on someone. The lack of a home is a rupture with society in terms of labor, culture, and economy—the very definition of social exclusion. Homelessness is an expression of supreme vulnerability.

Along with other organizations, RAIS pushed for the creation of a watchdog organization for hate crimes against the homeless called Hatento, and in collaboration with it, they carried out a study with a group of homeless people that arrived at alarming conclusions. According to the report, one out of every three homeless people has been insulted or mistreated, and one out of every five has suffered assault. The aggressors, in 30 percent of cases, are young people "out for a good time."

Caritas, FACIAM (the Federation of Associations of Centers for Integration and Assistance of the Marginalized), and FEPSH (the Federation of Entities Supporting the Homeless) initiated a campaign on November 27, 2016, with the motto "No one without a home," which stressed four fundamental points: that no one should sleep in the street; that no one should have to reside longer than necessary in emergency shelters; that no one should have to live longer than necessary in temporary housing; and that no young person should wind up homeless during the transition to independent living. According to the report of the Spanish branch of Caritas, *What Society Do We Live In?*, there are forty thousand homeless people in Spain.

This situation of defenselessness and vulnerability is already a result of aporophobia, of contempt for the poor, of generalized neglect. But like all attitudes, it can in certain situations lead to active rather than merely passive violence toward marginalized or potentially marginalized people. Nowadays, we refer to these by the striking term *hate crimes*. According to the Spanish Ministry of the Interior, a hate crime consists of "any criminal or administrative infraction committed against persons or property for reasons of race, ethnicity, religion, religious practices, age, disability, sexual orientation or identity, or any other similar factor, such as differences of ideology."[2] From the sociological perspective, it can be understood as "acts of violence, hostility, and intimidation committed toward persons chosen for their identity, which is perceived as *different* by those who act in this way."[3]

According to the Hatento report, two other social pathologies are intimately related to these types of crimes and must be distinguished from them: hateful incidents and hate speech.

Hateful incidents exist when there is evidence of contempt and mistreatment of people for belonging to a certain group

that does not rise to the level of a crime. Naturally, the fact
that these incidents are not crimes as such does not mean they
are insignificant, because they may degenerate into delinquency and because the purview of morals is broader than that
of the law. Contempt toward others, as well as actions based on
it, are the expression of flawed character and unacceptable
conditions.

Hate speech is as old as humanity itself. It consists of any form
of expression motivated by intolerance and intended to propa-
gate, incite, promote, or justify hatred toward certain groups.
It is discourse that attempts to stigmatize such groups and to
legitimate hostility toward them. The Committee of Ministers
of the Council of Europe defines it as "all forms of expressions that
spread, incite, promote or justify racial hatred, xenophobia, anti-
Semitism or other forms of hatred based on intolerance."[4]

The number of examples is overwhelming: xenophobia, the
extreme aversion to foreigners; homophobia, the hatred for
homosexual people; phobias related to Muslims, Christians, or
people of any other religion; and aporophobia, the contempt
for the poor and indigent, all form part of what may be more
broadly termed hate speech.

It is far from easy to distinguish between the term *hate speech*
and the crime designated as such. The essential difference is
that a crime is an act motivated by intolerance and a feeling of
superiority on the part of the aggressor that must fulfill at least
two criteria: it must be a degrading or aggressive act categorized
as a crime by a penal code, and it must be motivated by prejudice against a given social group.[5] The crime may be considered
a felony or misdemeanor.

Given the gray areas involved here, we will try for now to
tease out the common characteristics of those social pathologies considered to be motivated by hatred. In this connection,

it is useful to turn to one of La Fontaine's fables that André Glucksmann considers in his book *The Discourse of Hate*.

The Fable of the Wolf and the Lamb

A few months ago, at the end of my lecture at a conference on this subject, a colleague asked me if hate speech and hate crimes might not be an expression of a feeling of injustice, an indignant reaction on the part of a person who has been mistreated by members of a certain group or class. In part, he was right: it is common for people who have been harmed or offended to react violently. A reaction of this kind need not be an expression of unjustified hatred; it may rather be the result of a deep feeling of injustice that feeds a hatred that grows on its own and explodes in outrage. Injustices suffered personally or by groups feed a sense of humiliation and offense that gives rise to resentment that may crystallize into hatred. But the crimes and speech acts we are discussing do not refer to that kind of hatred, because the former are characterized precisely by targeting not people who have caused harm, but an entire group indiscriminately. An act of aggression may select an individual person, but it does so because of that person's belonging to a group. It attacks not *a person*, but rather *a beggar, a refugee, a woman, a Christian,* or *a Muslim*. La Fontaine's fable is illuminating in this regard as an example of the traits of this pathology.

As in many fables, the characters are two animals, in this case a wolf and a lamb who engage in dialogue. I say this, but really it's a monologue, with the wolf monopolizing the conversation while the lamb is a mere bit player, contributing just enough to allow his antagonist to go on talking.

"And last year I know that you slandered me."
"How can that be, if I wasn't yet born?"

Replied the lamb, "My mother still suckles me."
"If it isn't you, it's your brother then."
"I have no brother." "Then some relation:
For you are always plaguing me,
You, your dogs and shepherds too,
They tell me I should wreak revenge."
Whereupon the wolf dragged him through
The forest's depths and ate him up
Without further ado.

The wolf's words are a clear example of the meaning of hate speech, but they are also a hate crime, because they gather the characteristics that distinguish them from other kinds of speech and crime.

In principle, the speaker's words are directed against an individual, but not because that individual has caused any sort of damage; it is simply because he possesses a trait that marks him as a member of a given group. Here, *you* is different from *us. You* are the lambs in this fable; in other instances, *you* means people of another race (racism), another ethnic group (xenophobia), another sex (misogyny), a different religion (Christianophobia or Islamophobia), or an underprivileged social group (aporophobia).

The PSV fans didn't know the women asking for change in the Plaza Mayor, and neither they nor anyone else there enjoying the sun had been harmed by them, but the women belonged to a group—beggars—that these men must have considered worthy of contempt, to judge from their behavior.

This trait distinguishes hate crimes and hate speech from other violations: the victims are selected not for their personal identity, but because they belong to a group that possesses characteristics that give rise to repulsion and contempt in their aggressors. Any victim could be exchanged for any other member of the group who shares these characteristics. This is true of all people who profess a certain religion, share a certain ideology, form part of a certain race or ethnic or marginalized group disrespected by those who commit such crimes. There is no need for a prior relationship with the victim, who may be completely unknown to the aggressor, because the motive is contempt for a given characteristic rather than previous negative experiences.

The examples of such infractions are numberless. On October 11, 2016, *El País* reported that two individuals, twenty-eight and twenty-nine years old, had attempted to set fire to an indigent woman in Daroca, assaulting her as she slept out in the open. The neighbors came to the woman's aid, putting out the flames with buckets of water. Rarely do the aggressors in such cases face reprisal. Three more cases were examined in a 2015 article in *La Vanguardia*. The president of VOX in Cuenca was beaten by people who rejected her political positions and were so incapable of tolerating an ideology different from their own that they turned to violence. In Granada, a homeless man was beaten from aporophobia alone. And in Almeria, a young gay man was assaulted. The "reason"? Homophobia.

Misogyny, the aversion to women, which continues to persist in an astonishing number of ideologies, lies at the root of people's determination to cut off women's access to public life, to relegate them to their role in the family, the convent, or the brothel, to deny them permission to go outside without a man, to force them to seek permission to go abroad, to refuse them the right to vote, in many countries to massacre them for the simple fact of being women.[6] Not for being *a particular woman*, but for being *a woman*, period.

The same thing happens when a crime is committed against *a* gay person, *a* transgender person, *a* Muslim, *a* Jew, *a* Christian, or *a* poor person. The violence, obviously, is suffered by a person or a group of people, not on account of who they are as individuals, but because they are *one of* or *some of* a group. This conception of the individual as representative of a type seems to justify all sorts of infractions against individual persons, harming them physically and morally, destroying their self-esteem and their access to participation in the public sphere, even questioning their right to life.

Moreover, this happens everywhere, in universities, in companies, in politics, where competitors are eliminated not because they are incompetent, but because they are discredited and slandered for being *one of* a group deemed worthy of contempt. That is why it is essential to devote extraordinary effort to determining who in our daily lives actually counts as a victim—because often, it is far from clear.

Hate crimes may also stigmatize and degrade a group by attributing to it actions harmful for society, but difficult or impossible to confirm, often anchored in a remote past that has given rise to prejudice even if based only in rumor and hearsay.

Wolves can tell stories about shepherds and sheepdogs that discredit them all, even those not yet born. Much of the population rejects beggars because they've been told they belong to mafias and are a nuisance; anti-Semites have endless dark legends about the Jews; those who hate religions remember the key points of inquisitions of the past and keep suspiciously silent about present-day inquisitions that have nothing whatsoever to do with religion. The question is hence not one of a given lamb, beggar, Jew, or Christian with a first and last name, but of the dissolution of the person into the collective.

The collective falls under the crosshairs of hatred thanks to dark myths about them invented by people who believe society ought to feel hatred for them. At times, these even promote violent actions against their members. "They tell me I should

wreak revenge" is a message of the obedience the wolf submits to.[7]
Even attempting to summarize the history of violence against
vulnerable minorities would result in an endless chronicle.

Those who reject political refugees and poor immigrants say
that they are coming to steal jobs, take advantage of social safety
nets, and, more recently, that their ranks include terrorists sent
by the Islamic State planning the kind of attacks that took place
in Paris, Nice, Brussels, Frankfurt, and Berlin. Unfortunately,
Donald Trump is not the only one who thinks this way.

The Tunisian Anis Amri, suspect in the massacre in Berlin of
December 18, 2016, gave ammunition to aporophobic and xenophobic people both, as a refugee who arrived in Lampedusa
in 2011 and was taken in by a family because he was still a minor.
In cases like his, the reaction of parties and individuals inclined
to close the borders to poor people from elsewhere is to spread
suspicion and rejection of all immigrants and refugees who arrive in our countries in inhumane conditions. This is the distinctive element of hate crimes: they select their victims not for
who they are, but for the group they belong to.

Whoever engages in hate speech or commits a hate crime is
convinced that there exists a *structural inequality* between himself and the victim, and within it, he is in the superior position.
Such a person employs hate speech to maintain that feeling of
superiority. In this way, he embraces an ideology in the Marxian
sense of a deformed and deforming vision of reality that allows
the better-situated group to strengthen its *structural superiority*
while maintaining the victims in a subordinate position.[8]

The challenge, then, is not only building a pluralistic society
in which people are entitled to a minimum of justice and can
opt for competing visions of a full or good life. True, it isn't easy
to organize life in common in morally plural societies; accom-
modating diversity is always a painstaking task.[9] Hatred is not

a matter of simple difference, but of the conviction that there exists a structural hierarchy in which the aggressor occupies the upper rungs while the aggressed remain at the bottom.

This makes it impossible to guarantee a minimum of justice because there are no equal relations, no recognition of the dignity of the aggressed and the respect they deserve. Hate crimes are a flagrant violation of the supreme principle of modern ethics as formulated by Kant in the second formulation of the categorical imperative: "Act in such a way that you treat humanity, whether in your own person or in the person of any other, never merely as a means to an end, but always at the same time as an end." The aggressor, however, treats his victim as a means, failing to recognize his equal claims to humanity and dignity—as an object rather than as a subject who must be taken into account.

Another of the characteristics of hate speech, whether or not it includes incitement to violence, is its near or total absence of argumentation. It does not attempt to debate, but only to express and spread contempt. "Without further ado," just as the wolf eats the lamb in the fable.

Hate crimes make equality impossible, and thus call into question a key value in democratic societies, one that Ronald Dworkin describes as the sovereign virtue. The path to ridding ourselves of hate speech and hate crimes is the establishment of equality through formal and informal education and the creation of political and economic institutions that bring it into being. Without an awareness of equality, which must be at once rational and sentient, people's dignity will inevitably be violated, and it will be impossible to build a just society. But the government, the law, and the penal system all have a role here, too, in punishing crimes of this kind. The function of the law is not only punishment and rehabilitation, but also communication.

State and Civil Society, a Necessary Collaboration

"The risk of becoming a victim of hate or of a hate crime for the homeless is greatest when coming into contact with another person who does not believe them deserving of respect and is willing to act against them in consequence. Those who commit hate crimes motivated by aporophobia are the only ones responsible for their actions."[10]

In 2016, the Spanish Ministry of the Interior published its third *Report on Incidents Related to Hate Crimes in Spain*. The record of such incidents is more exhaustive than ever, as police agencies have learned better to detect infractions of this type. One of the greatest obstacles here has been the difficulty of verifying when an act is motivated by hatred, aversion, or rejection to such a degree that it can be classified among the felonies and misdemeanors known as hate crimes. The report's objective is to minimize the risks suffered by certain vulnerable groups, to raise awareness of their plight in society, to promote a zero-tolerance approach, and to encourage victims to place their trust in law enforcement.

The report declares expressly that it is the responsibility of the state to protect the most vulnerable members of society, among them victims of discrimination and hatred. It describes aporophobia as "hatred or rejection of the poor" and reprimands those words or actions that express "hatred, repugnance, or hostility to the poor, the indigent, and the homeless."[11]

An evolution is observable in the ministry's three reports on this social pathology. According to the Statistical Yearbook of the Ministry of the Interior, in 2013 a total of 1,172 hate crimes were recorded in 2013, 4 of them instances of aporophobia; in 2014, of 1,285 hate crimes, 11 were motivated by aporophobia; in

2015, of the 1,328 hate crimes on record, 17 were examples of aporophobia.

Hatento has reasonably questioned whether this is the true number of such incidents, or whether it is likely that victims do not report such crimes, believing that they will not be listened to; whether they might fear reprisal; whether they are unaware that these incidents constitute a punishable crime; whether they feel guilty themselves, believing that their situation provokes such infractions; or whether their vulnerable status leads them to distrust or fear the police. Moreover, the police struggle to identify crimes of this kind, and judges face many difficulties in determining if an infraction is indeed motivated by hatred, rejection, or aversion to the destitute.

There is another set of data from several institutions that is essential for understanding the profile of aggressors. According to the National Coalition for the Homeless in the United States, studies conducted over the past fifteen years show that 85 percent of aggressors are under thirty years of age and 93 percent of them are male.

Between December 1, 2014 and April 30, 2015, Hatento carried out a series of interviews with the homeless.[12] In doing so, they kept in mind two key points: first, that a structural inequality exists between aggressors and victims that obliges the victim to adopt a subordinate position, and second, that victims of such aggression or humiliation tend to perceive the cause of these acts as lying in their own situation of marginalization or homelessness. Hatento interviewed 261 people. Among their findings were the following:[13]

47.1 percent of those interviewed were victims of an incident or crime related to aporophobia during the time that they were homeless. For every ten such incidents, six occurred at night or in the early morning hours, generally when the victims were asleep. 87 percent of those involved in these incidents were male, 57 percent of them between eighteen and thirty-five years old. In 28.4 percent of cases, those responsible were young men out partying. The most frequent aggressors were young men, in 38.3 percent of cases.

Only 15 out of the 114 people who described one of these incidents in detail reported it to the police, and none mentioned that this had resulted in an eventual guilty verdict. Seventy percent of those who did not file a report stated that there was no point in doing so, and 11 percent were afraid of repercussions from their aggressors.

In the face of such data, we must insist on the importance of hate crimes being recognized and sanctioned with penalties that correspond to their gravity. Not only because of the punitive or rehabilitative function that the law serves, but also for the pedagogical purpose of communicating that society is unwilling to tolerate actions that violate the values that give it meaning and identity, among them the respect for the equal dignity of individual persons.

The above-cited reports highlight the importance of training the police to prevent these actions to the extent that this is possible; but when the damage is done, they should be able to detect when aggression is not an ordinary crime, but an instance of aporophobia; and they should attend to the victims as carefully as possible, letting them know they have society's support. Judges' behavior in these cases should likewise be lucid and balanced, with an eye toward increasing society's sensitivity toward them so that they may be seen as what they are: unacceptable.

Civil society organizations such as those we have mentioned here have an essential role in denouncing, revealing the facts, and proposing solutions. The state and the legal apparatus must be on the lookout for injustices and support the victims, but without the contributions of civil society, they are not enough. We must push for a home for everyone, so no one is obliged to beg or to be enslaved by mafias. Poverty must be eradicated, inequality reduced, and the impression of common dignity reinforced.

The Poor Person Is in All Cases an Unprofitable Person

Aporophobia is distinct from other types of hatred or rejection for several reasons, among them that involuntary poverty is not an identity trait per se. Even if identity is negotiated in dialogue with one's social surroundings, which are dynamic rather than static, race and ethnicity, however difficult these traits are to pin down, do contribute to defining it, as do sex and sexual identity; whereas religious affiliation or lack thereof represent personal choices no one should be obliged to accept or renounce.

Involuntary poverty, however, is neither a personal identity nor a choice. Those who suffer from it may be resigned to it and may come to accept it as the framework within which to judge their minimal possibilities for ameliorating their lives. These forms of alms taking, accepted thanks to "adaptive preferences," must be denounced for maintaining in acquiescent poverty people who are not even properly aware of their condition, and poverty, being a social ill produced by natural or social causes, is something that ought to be eliminated in the twenty-first century. It has taken hundreds of years to arrive at this realization, hundreds of years of evolution from the belief that the poor are responsible for their situation to recognizing that society itself is responsible for eradicating the causes of poverty.

It follows that eliminating aporophobia demands educating people and creating economic and political institutions that attempt to eliminate poverty by building equality-based institutions, because asymmetrical relations lie at the very base of aporophobia. In principle, poverty signifies a lack of the means necessary for survival, but it is something more than that. We agree with Amartya Sen that poverty is a lack of freedom, the impossibility of carrying out life plans a person has come to cherish through rational consideration. Sen and Martha Nussbaum propose that human beings must be able to exercise certain basic capacities in order to see through their life plans. We have examined above aporophobia as a criminal act, but it is also an attitude of *contempt and rejection toward each member of the lowest rung* in economic and social terms.

There seems to be an innate tendency in inhumanity to take the side of the better situated, those who may offer some benefit, and to leave aside the *aporoi*, who present few advantages and cannot even avenge themselves against the offenses they have experienced, and this is an immense source of unjust suffering. Developing awareness of this, and asking whether this is the kind of people we want to be around and to be, is tantamount to asking whether we want to live in a humane or inhumane society.

For this reason, we must discover the deep roots of aporophobia, try to investigate its causes, and understand whether they are part of human nature—whether the poor will always and inevitably be subject to contempt and rejection, or whether there are ways for individuals and societies to modify these and understand that hostility toward the poor violates the most basic principles of humanity. This is a challenge for moral education, which must count on the support of political and economic institutions, because education takes place not only in school, in the university, and in the family, but also via institutions and the mass media.

To start with, we will examine the pathology of hate speech, which at times is an incitement to hate crimes and in other cases, constitutes a hate crime in and of itself.

Chapter 3

Hate Speech

An Unavoidable Debate

The need to debate what has been called, fortunately or unfortunately, hate speech has been a salient issue in recent years in light of such incidents as the *Charlie Hebdo* massacre in January of 2015, when twelve people were murdered after cartoons mocking Mohammad appeared in the journal's pages; the drawings in that same magazine comparing the 296 dead in the Amatrice earthquake with Italian dishes; the xenophobic and aporophobic discourses of populist parties in Europe during the refugee crisis; the aporophobic and xenophobic campaign of Donald Trump, with its insulting rhetoric toward Mexicans; ISIS's videos with their threats of death and conquest; and many other violent expressions distributed through cyberspace.[1]

Though addressed to different groups and reflecting a wide variety of attitudes (irony, satire, contempt, incitement to violence, credible threats), hate speech is as old as humanity and as widespread as culture itself. But there are three new tendencies in relation to it in democratic society: first, hate speech has come under the purview of the legal system and may be considered a hate crime; second, it has spread into cyberspace, where it is virtually impossible to control; third, mature societies have come to question explicitly whether hate speech may constitute an obstacle for democratic life in common.

The epicenter of debates around hate speech in democratic societies lies in the conflict between the exercise of free expression on the part of those engaged in presumptively harmful speech acts and those this speech may harm and whom society has a duty to protect. Freedom of expression is a basic right in open societies and must be defended and reinforced; but it is not an absolute right, and limits to it exist where it may violate other basic rights or entitlements.

For example, Section 20.4 of the Spanish Constitution affirms expressly with regard to the freedom of expression and information that "these freedoms are limited by respect for the rights recognised in this Part, by the legal provisions implementing it, and especially by the right to honour, to privacy, to the own image and to the protection of youth and childhood."[2] As these terms in practice are highly ambiguous, limits must be established through debates clarifying these limits' nature and what criteria ought to codify them.

This is an urgent desideratum in order not to deprive the weak and helpless, the *aporoi* of all kinds, of necessary protections. In this chapter, therefore, we will attempt to confront this problem and propose a solution that goes beyond the apparent dilemma of restricted versus unrestricted freedom of expression, showing that this, like other apparently irresolvable impasses in human life, is a problem that demands a head-on solution. An interaction of law and ethics is necessary to overcome the inevitable conflicts that occur when the question is examined from an exclusively juridical point of view.

Freedom of Expression or the Right to Self-Esteem?

Hate crimes and hate speech share the following commonalities: they are directed against an individual for belonging to a group; they stigmatize a given group as an object worthy of hatred; they denigrate groups with narratives or spurious scientific theories that presume to demonstrate their worthiness of contempt; they evince the structural inequality between those who proffer hate speech and the stigmatized group (us versus them); and when words transcend insults and become hate speech, they avoid argumentation in favor of justifications for hatred or incitement to violence.

A crime is a felony or misdemeanor.[3] Speech may rise to the level of a crime, and for this reason prompts the following questions from the judicial point of view: (1) What kind of speech can be characterized as hate speech, and what is the branch of law best equipped to sanction it?[4] (2) How should freedom of expression—a basic right in liberal societies—be balanced against the right of every person to self-esteem, peaceful integration in society, and recognition?[5] (3) Does freedom of expression deserve constitutional protection with regard to the promulgation of any idea whatsoever, even those that are repulsive from the point of view of human dignity or that clash with the values put forth in the constitution? Keep in mind, a distinction must be made between hate speech (which is generally not protected by freedom of expression) and offensive or unpopular speech (which generally is).

These questions demand a clear response, principally because open societies must not dispense with that freedom of expression that allows different voices to express themselves and be heard. Prohibiting certain kinds of expression is a hallmark of totalitarianism, one we in Spain are well familiar with and one that persists in countries like Venezuela, China, and North Korea.[6] At the same time, freedom of speech has limits when it infringes upon legally protected rights, as hate speech sometimes does. When it does, it becomes a crime that must be recognized and penalized above all in order to indicate that it conflicts with the values of the broader society.

And yet, as specialists in these matters have noted, speech acts that may be construed as apologizing or inciting hatred or discrimination and that in this way offend against constitutionally protected rights and values are rarely punished for reasons both objective and subjective.[7] With regards to the first, speech, in order to be deemed illicit, must violate constitutionally protected rights or values or contain an incitement to violence— offensive opinion alone is not enough. And experience shows that determining when a concrete instance of speech incites violence is a matter of interpretation. This is perhaps why what matters decisively in this regard is that which Rawls calls "burdens of justice," the most important of which is the evaluation, in complex cases, of the facts at hand, taking into account the experiences acquired throughout our history; but as histories differ, so interpretations are weighed down by differing evaluations. Another matter worth considering here is political pressure, and particularly the sway exerted by political correctness.[8] With it, powerful social groups manage to mark as illicit speech that attacks them or that they consider intolerable. There is, of course, the opposite case of groups that lack power in society and are attacked in discourses that are considered the simple exercise of freedom of expression. Again, this is deeply relevant to aporophobia. Whoever lacks the power necessary to demand a reply in the form of recompense or vengeance cannot presume their self-esteem will be protected. Strangely enough, none of the major works on this subject examines speech acts directed against the truly poor.[9]

The difficulty of determining when hate speech grades into a hate crime has led some others to stress that legal sanctions must be reserved as a last resort and that other, less wide-ranging but perhaps more effective corrective measures should be looked into, such as damages in civil suits.[10] This is surely an avenue worth exploring, but it is not without its own complexities.

Even from the subjective point of view, it is far from easy to determine when hate is the motive for a criminal act, and the subjective aspect of such acts is another reason why this sort of crime often goes unpunished. The worry thus exists that, getting lost in subjective details in the attempt to determine whether a given instance rises to the level of criminality, we may forget the harms wrought by hate speech on individuals and communities. For this reason, many advise against an exclusive focus on penal law.[11]

In my view, however, another path must be explored, one complementary to rather than distinct from those already mentioned, which transforms the question by examining it in light of the ethical roots of democratic open societies.

The Construction of Radical Democracy

In his article "Hate Speech and Adjectivized Democracy: Tolerant, Intransigent, Militant?", Miguel Revenga distinguishes between three models of democracy as a response to the question of how far a society is willing to go in its defense of freedom of expression.[12] Whereas hate speech may cause harm, freedom of expression is for many authors the basic marker of how democratic a country is.[13]

Following Revenga, the model of a tolerant democracy would be the United States, where the First Amendment has been interpreted to protect virtually all forms of speech.[14] The Constitution commands the state to protect liberty even in very exceptional cases, and tolerance is considered an essential virtue.[15] Paradigmatic of this way of understanding liberty is the Skokie case. In 1978, a neo-Nazi party overseen by Frank Collin sought permission to stage a protest in the Jewish-majority village of Skokie, Illinois, to promote, among other ideas, denial of the Holocaust. Local authorities attempted to block them, but the Supreme Court upheld their right under the precept of freedom of expression.

An intransigent democracy would follow the European model, more inclined to limit individual freedom of expression in questions of hate speech. Lying in the background of this disposition is the experience of the Holocaust, which had its origin in the tolerance of populist and presumptively scientific discourses filled with direct and indirect incitements to violence that led to systematic, state-organized murder, and also the history of the European wars of religion. Another important aspect is the honor culture with deep roots in Europe, kept alive in the legal prohibition on insults, which the Spanish Supreme Court has established lack constitutional protection.

The term *militant democracy* comes from two articles published by Karl Loewenstein in 1937 under the title "Militant Democracy and Fundamental Rights."[16] For Loewenstein, there is a need for a type of democracy insulated against the failures of weak democracies like the Weimar Republic in 1919. The constitution of a militant democracy must contain clauses that impede its reform and forestall the legalization of parties opposed to constitutional order. In Loewenstein's judgment, the experience of National Socialism justifies such measures. This type of democracy would also demand citizens adhere to constitutional principles—and to my mind, this exceeds the functions of the law.

Another possible alternative to weak democracy would be the *strong democracy* proposed in 1984 by Benjamin Barber. According to him, the flagging liberal democracy of the Weimer Republic led the citizenry to disinvest from politics. Politically enervated, the people were fascinated by the strong option Hitler represented. Once more, the pied piper had seduced the masses. As an antidote, Barber proposes encouraging citizens to engage in public life through the kind of participatory democracy advocated by Rousseau and Walt Whitman.[17]

A strong democracy, however, cannot be a unitary democracy that brings together the citizenry through a marker of elemental unity like blood or ideology. Participation on its own is not an unalloyed good: instead, one must know the state's principles and goals. Under National Socialism, these were poisonous; hence Barber's strong democracy takes pluralism as its basis, along with the kind of dialogue and deliberation that allows a transition from liberal democracy's aggregationism, reigned over by the sum of individual wills, to a common will. Deliberation allows a shift from "I prefer this" to "We want the world to be like this."

Each of these models has bright spots and shadows, and over time, they have come together. Tolerant democracy defends the principle of freedom of expression in the belief that the best ideas will win out in the marketplace, while bad ones will disappear without any need for prohibitions.[18] This faith may or may not be successful in the long term, but in the short term, it may cause harm by infringing upon others. Whether or not speech incites violence against them, it violates the "freedom of the moderns," understood as freedom to act without interference.[19] It must be said that the virtue of tolerance is always superior to intolerance, but it risks fostering intolerant speech acts. This is the basis of my contention that active respect is the virtue that actually triumphs over intolerance. A person who respects others is extremely unlikely to promulgate intolerant speech acts that may harm them.

Intransigent democracy may excessively limit freedom of expression and substitute a culture of honor for one of self-esteem, that basic good valued as highly in the Anglo-Saxon tradition as in the European, so much so that Rawls considers it one of his primary goods. Primary goods are those any person would wish to have irrespective of his individual life plan. Everyone would like to enjoy certain rights and possess certain economic means and self-esteem, which allows one to trust one's own ability to carry out engaging projects throughout one's life. European legal codes may recognize the right to honor, but this value is something of an anachronism in the twentieth century, while self-esteem is broadly recognized.

Active respect—a virtue that works against damaging others' self-esteem—is the key to neutralizing hate speech.

In principle, militant democracy appears a highly attractive option, because it implicates the citizenry in the project of constructing a democratic society, but it has at least two grave limitations: (a) the inalterable nature of the constitution, which is intolerable because all texts are subject to reform so long as constitutional principles are preserved; and (b) the demand that the citizenry actively comply with constitutional principles. Can the law actually ask citizens to commit actively to democratic principles, or only to not violating these principles?[20]

Having arrived at this point, it is useful to recall Kant's distinction between political freedom and moral freedom. Political freedom is external freedom, which regulates relations between persons, and its limitations exist where harm can be caused to others. The state may turn to coercion to force citizens to respect the freedom of others irrespective of the coerced person's belief in the sovereignty of the law. Moral freedom is internal liberty, personal autonomy, the capacity of each subject to dictate laws to himself and to oblige himself to given actions.[21] Its domain is self-compulsion and the cultivation of personal virtue not as an obligation, but as a private pursuit. Kant would add with relation to liberty that the law cannot be adduced as a motive to action, as its purpose is to describe what conforms to the law rather than to teach virtue itself.[22]

The citizens of an open society therefore cannot be obliged to adopt legal principles as a motive to action, but only to avoid violating those principles, and so a militant democracy of the type we have described is not sufficient. Where the law doesn't reach, civic ethics can and must take over, and it is this that is indispensable for a functioning democracy.

The cultivation of ethics is a responsibility for society as a whole, which must transmit the exemplary nature of certain figures and shape organizations and institutions in ethical ways through formal and informal education, schools, families, and communication media.

Hegel was correct in his belief that it was insufficient to prescribe that which ought to be, that morals ought to be incorporated in the institutions, habits, and customs of a society, and he called this incorporation, which also draws private life into its ambit, *Sittlichkeit*, generally translated as "ethical life" or "ethical order."[23]

We may distinguish three great ethical stages in history, each of which integrates two types of ethical theories, one idealistic—calling for innovative proposals—and one realist—determined to impress ethical precepts upon existing institutions. The first stage would be that of Plato and Aristotle; the second, that of Kant and Hegel; the third, that of the dialogue between Apel and Habermas in the twentieth century, which has come to be integrated into the institutions of democratic societies thanks to the revolution of applied ethics—that is, through the ethics of human development, economics and business, communications, politics, education, and the professions, and bioethics and cyberethics.[24] All of these impregnate assorted spheres of social life and instate moral demands the fulfillment of which requires a manifestation of values and a cultivation of virtues understood as the perfection of character. Their progress consists in reinforcing in all these fields the intersubjective ties that bind members of society through dialogic and democratic ethics.[25]

It is here where we see that the conflict between hate speech and freedom of expression exceeds the capacities of juridical solutions and demands the invocation of democratic *Sittlichkeit*: because the law functions exclusively through legal and social coercion, the limitations of which are more than evident.

The cultivation of democratic ethics requires that liberty be deemed sacred: specifically an *equal liberty* achieved through dialogue and mutual recognition of freedom, not among atomized individuals who come together in order to make common decisions, but among those conscious of being persons embedded in relations. This is why the supreme virtue is the active respect for dignity, which assumes tolerance but also goes beyond it, committing to not doing harm and not breaking ties to others, who possess dignity and not merely material value.

The Poverty of Hate Speech

Neither the word "hate" nor the word "speech" adequately describes what hate speech is, and analyzing the reasons why not is essential to bringing to light its conceptual poverty.

With regards to the term "hate," this deeply rooted emotion does not always correspond to the motivations for the kinds of speech and crimes we are here describing. In the common sense, we take hate to be a very intense emotion, a violent feeling of repulsion against people or things accompanied by the desire to do harm or to see harm done to them. Glucksmann affirms that hate is real and that it is destructive, and he is right. But hate speech also refers to less radical forms of aversion and rejection that nonetheless do great harm to those who suffer them. In these cases, we may be dealing with a mere antipathy or aversion accompanied by the desire to see their object made to suffer; and at times, the most adequate description is a phobia, an exaggerated form of aversion or rejection.

This is true of aporophobia, which shuns the poor person because poverty is an unpleasant reality and the poor person is problematic and seems somehow contagious. At issue here is not only economic poverty, but any form of deprivation that leaves a person helpless and with nowhere to turn, subject to criticism, threats, contempt, or mockery. This is common in politics, business, universities, schools, factories, and anywhere else, a result of the Matthew Effect, whereby "For to every one who has will more be given, and he will have abundance; but from him who has not, even what he has will be taken away." A poor person in this sense is one who lacks power in a given time and place, and such a person will be the objects of speech acts embodying aversion, rejection, even hate, expressed by the better-situated and their inevitable lackeys.

Naturally, judges require criteria by which to determine whether a speech act is motivated by hatred and whether it therefore constitutes a crime, but from the ethical perspective, whoever rejects or denigrates from a position of power of any kind shatters the possibility of just and amicable life in common, and degrades himself by breaking his bond to the humiliated or offended party.

The term "speech" is problematic as well, because it may be used to describe insults or outbursts that do not rise to the level of a discourse. Nonetheless, we will accept it provisionally here in order to critique discourses based in hatred on three principle points.

First, hate speech is monological and not dialogical. The wolf issues his diatribe against the lamb and is uninterested in hearing a response. The party uttering it does not deem his listener a valid interlocutor or a subject with a right to reply and enter into dialogue; instead he sees him as an object lacking any claim to respect.

Even from the linguistic point of view, such a posture is unacceptable, because whoever addresses another person through language, even through gestures, takes for granted that a tie of some kind exists between them, that the listener is capable of understanding, and this capability brings with it a right to reply, to agree, or to disagree. These capacities are the claim of autonomous subjects and are incompatible with heteronymous objects.

As the *Theory of Communicative Action* states, speech is a kind of communicative action in which interlocutors must understand one another because, were things otherwise, communication would not exist. Speech lacks meaning if a minimum of understanding isn't sought.[26] Every communicative action, even that addressed by the wolf to the lamb, enacts an inevitable pragmatic supposition that is the motive for engaging in it: there exists a logical-pragmatic link between interlocutors that is at the same time a relation of mutual recognition. To deny the listener's claim to this, to treat him as an object rather than a subject, means breaking the intersubjective bond presupposed by human language and affirming the meaninglessness of language. In this way, it is a performative contradiction that treats the interlocutor as an object by means of a discourse that can only be directed to speaking subjects. The bond broken by the one party at the semantic level exists, whether he wants it to or not, at the pragmatic level.[27]

Second, hate speech, unlike ordinary speech, may harm the people it is directed toward whether or not it incites others to murder, harm, or otherwise prejudice them. As many authors have noted, communicative action is action, however much this principle is forgotten.[28] *Speaking is acting*, it is carrying out an action, and it is capable of producing damage on its own. Irrespective of its possible criminality, *from the ethical point of view* it is harmful to stigmatize people, to condemn them to exclusion or the loss of reputation or to deprive them of the right to participate in society, and this renders just life in common impossible.

Third, the mere fact of establishing *asymmetrical relations*, relations of *radical inequality* between "us" and "them," violates the most basic principles of the democratic ethos. Democratic societies are hardly possible without democratic character, and certain values are essential to that character, among them freedom and liberty—this is the great heritage of the democratic tradition, and the overarching project of radical democracies, democracies concerned with the root, with humanity, is the construction of equal liberty.

Asymmetrical discourses express an absence of that *mutual recognition* that is the key to just social life. This insight appears throughout a philosophical tradition that begins with Hegel and thrives in contemporary discourse ethics as expressed by Karl-Otto Apel and Jürgen Habermas and expanded upon by such authors as Charles Taylor, Paul Ricœur, Axel Honneth, Jesús Conill, Domingo García-Marzá, Juan Carlos Siurana, and myself.[29] As Taylor writes, the victory of the executioner consists of forcing his victim to hate himself as others do.

I cannot avoid citing here Karl-Otto Apel's splendid text, *Toward a Transformation of Philosophy*:

> All beings who are capable of linguistic communication must be recognized as persons since in all their actions and utterances they are potential participants in a discussion, and the unlimited justification of thought cannot dispense with any participant, nor with any of his potential contributions to a discussion.[30]

The reciprocal recognition of persons as valid interlocutors is the key to any discourse that would call itself rational. Hate speech breaks with this human intersubjectivity which, as Hannah Arendt says, must never be harmed.

Freedom Is Built through Active Respect

Confronting the problem of hate speech from the juridical perspective alone places us in the difficult position of determining when the criminal nature of a speech act requires infringing upon freedom of expression. These two appear locked in a zero-sum game that makes the conflict between them irresolvable.

A totalitarian society is one that suppresses freedom of expression, closes newspapers, publishers, and communications media, and imprisons dissidents. Open societies, on the contrary, consider freedom of expression an inalienable right that must be reinforced and encouraged. But if they wish truly to be democratic, they must do this while stressing the importance of mutual recognition of dignity among people who have a right to respect and to self-esteem. Neither active respect nor freedom of expression can be weakened or set aside, and practicing both is the task of civic ethics, which are based in the mutual recognition that constitutes the bedrock of democratic societies upon which the edifice of the law is built.[31]

Civic ethics in a democratic and pluralistic society divide responsibility for concrete persons, those who constitute the axis of any and all dialogues about the nature of justice, between institutions and persons. Hate speech weakens the comity, displaces intersubjectivity, and breaks interpersonal ties. The quality of a democratic society must be judged by the degree to which it achieves mutual recognition and respect for individuals' dignity, not by the degree to which it allows one party to harm another without incurring criminal penalties. Individual freedom of expression is not the sole barometer for measuring democracy. When mutual respect flags, democracy is eclipsed by an unrestrained individualist libertarianism, which is not the same thing as the appreciation of individual liberty proper to democratic societies.

It is not possible to maintain respect for the individual or defend the social basis of self-esteem without morally empowering citizens to consider their fellow citizens as people, as valid interlocutors, worthy of respect, rather than as beings that deserve only hatred, contempt, and rejection for the color of their skin, their race, their ethnic group, their religious convictions, their ideology, their handicaps, or their poverty.

Poverty is key in all of these cases, because societies do not simply reject any skin color, race, ethnic group, religion, or ideology—rather, hate speech is aimed against those that find themselves in a position of weakness.

Aporophobia is inevitably at the root of speech acts that target those in subordinate positions.

Chapter 4

Our Brain Is Aporophobic

Take xenophobia, the fear of foreigners. It's completely
natural. People prefer people who look and sound like them;
although contemptible, it is common to dislike outsiders.
Our policies work to cement into place the most enlightened
ideas of humanity to surmount the basest facets of human
nature. . . . It took a long time to get there, but the fact that
we did demonstrates that we are a flexible society that can
improve our standards based on better understanding.[1]

We Have a Dream

If we asked liberal democratic societies what their shared ideals
are, they would likely declare, following Martin Luther King,
that they have a dream, and this dream could likely be described
as follows.

In the political realm, we would like a democracy capable of
embodying the values of liberty and equality that give meaning
and legitimacy to this form of political organization. This might
be a deliberative democracy at the national scale, a world democracy even, capable of distributing common goods justly

and establishing clear, firm laws for a global economy. An inclusive democracy, even.

As for the economy, we would desire an ethical economy, prepared to fulfill its duties by helping to create good societies, in line with the affirmations of Nobel Prizewinner Amartya Sen.[2] The goal of the economy would be to create wealth with equality, eradicate poverty, and reduce injustice.

Encouraging economic citizenship would be another project of this common dream, encouraging citizens to become agents in decisions about what is produced, for whom, and why.[3]

Society would be civil, vibrant, with an appreciation for private life but a desire to participate in public matters and to commit to the common good.

This dream would likewise envision a morally pluralistic society, in which different ethical systems and different visions of the good life would coexist, sharing a basic idea of justice not subject to renunciation. Religious and secular ethics would contribute to visions of a happy life.[4] People could share their societies' basic visions of justice without renouncing their own cultural backgrounds, in line with the project of an intercultural society at the national and global level.[5]

The model of citizenship in everyday life would be that of the social citizen who sees his first- and second-generation rights protected within his political community.[6] Nation-states would be social justice states capable of protecting these rights.[7]

The European Union would become an authentic supranational union, recover the social project at its root, and develop into a Europe of citizens and politicians rather than simply of merchant powers. Hospitality toward refugees and immigrants would once more be its immutable watchword.

With respect to the irreversible phenomenon of globalization, it would proceed in the framework of a global governance capable of protecting a cosmopolitan citizenship.[8]

The horizon of this dream would be a cosmopolitan society in which all people would know and feel themselves to be citizens.

Naturally, aporophobia, xenophobia, racism, and homophobia would be excluded from this society because mutual respect for the dignity of persons demands as much. And stewardship of nature would be the final step in this world, which appears utopian but which would at least be acceptable in principle to liberal democratic societies. And yet, strangely, what actually happens is light years away from such principles.

A Gulf between Declarations and Deeds

We live in a contradictory world as regards politics, the economy, science, and social organization. In all these fields, the declarations of the most important institutions exist at what Lawrence Kohlberg would call the "post-conventional" level in terms of their development of moral consciousness. This psychologist of moral development, who worked in close collaboration with John Rawls, proposed to analyze the degree of development of moral consciousness in individuals by examining the development of the consciousness of justice. Much criticism of this identification of morals and justice soon ensued, arguing that benevolence and passion were also essential to the moral universe, and Kohlberg did respond to them; but for what concerns us here, the Universal Declaration of Human Rights and the treaties founded upon it, the sense of justice is critical.

Kohlberg detected three levels in the ontogenetic development of individual moral consciousness. In the first, people consider just what favors them; in the second, they hold to be just that which coincides with the norms of the community (communitarianism); in the third, which is the highest level of moral maturity, people reflect on justice and injustice with reference to humanity as a whole (universalism). Later, Jürgen Habermas would outline his theory of social evolution, taking as a model for his notion of phylogenetic or social moral consciousness the levels Kohlberg analyzed in individuals.

Kohlberg himself notes that in the pluralist and democratic societies of North America and much of Latin America and Europe there is a gulf between the ethics that legitimates economic and political institutions and the judgment of the citizenry. While institutions legitimate themselves through a defense of human rights and the moral values of the Enlightenment, thus situating themselves at a universalist moral level, the people who work in these institutions and the citizenry are at the conventional or preconventional level of moral judgment.[9]

We may say then that there exist in these societies a universalist moral social consciousness and civic ethics that gives meaning to political institutions while personal actions are selfish or communitarian and serve to benefit individuals or groups. And so ethics as written and spoken of, the public ethics transmitted through education at schools and universities, which alleges to govern decision-making in the codes, committees, and commissions of bioethics, businesses, the public administration, or political parties, embraces human rights, Enlightenment values, and increasingly care for the earth.

The moral consciousness of Western societies has evolved throughout its history: slavery has been outlawed, as have unequal treatment on the basis of race, ethnicity, sex, sexual preference, or income. Many groups describe this evolution in terms of the widening of the circle of those considered worthy of moral consideration. First those were male citizens; after the abolition of slavery, they included the former slaves, and slowly blacks and women were able to actively enter the citizenry; and now the circle is reaching nonhuman animals. At the level of written morals, of declarations, it is undeniable that diversity never justifies unequal treatment, and negative discrimination is forbidden.

This is the morality that José Luis Aranguren calls "thought morality." We consider that the equivalent of "written morality" as contained in constitutions, textbooks, and various codes of ethics.[10] Included here would be the 1948 Universal Declaration of Human Rights and the United Nations' vital commitments in the Millennium Development Goals (2000) and the Sustainable Development Goals (2015). These embrace the goals of eradicating hunger and ending extreme poverty and unjust inequality in its various forms as a declared objective within their thought, written, or declared morality. We must remember, too, that a declaration is not a neutral discourse, but a form of commitment.

It is, then, disheartening to see the contrast between such declarations and the morality of persons and institutions in practice. This may not be a new phenomenon, but rather one made more visible today thanks to the constant flow of information from news media and the internet.

In our *declarations*, we say that another world is possible, even necessary, because the one we have is less than human beings deserve. And I would add that the necessary is possible and must be made real. But to achieve this, we must understand why this gulf between declarations and realizations exists, why we want one world and build another, why we speak constantly of the importance of building inclusive democracies and enormous numbers of people continue to be left out.

Three Versions of Radical Evil

This asymmetry between words and actions has been called moral weakness (*akrasia*). Moral weakness is present when someone forms a moral judgment, such as "smoking is bad for me," but lights another cigarette when it is time to act. This weakness of the will is perfectly expressed in the Latin maxim "*Video meliora proboque deteriora sequor*" (I see what is best and I do what is worst), which Ovid has Medea express as follows: "But a strange power draws me to him against my will. Love urges one thing: reason another. I see, and I desire the better: I follow the worse."[111] The same sentiment is evident in the Epistles of Saint Paul: "For what I would, that do I not; but what I hate, that do I."[12]

This is not just an individual ill, but a social one. Both people and societies believe certain things are best when they speak, but act in a contrary manner. How are we to explain this moral weakness in society?

Some religions, the Jewish and Christian ones among them, find the response in the original sin committed by Adam and Eve, passed down to the entire human race, and only absolvable through divine grace. This explanation of original sin entered into philosophy in a secular form in what some authors call the "doctrine of radical evil." A well-known example is that of Kant, who understands radical evil as the natural tendency of people to choose selfishness above moral duty. Following Augustine and Luther, Kant arrives at his famous formulation that from the crooked timber of humanity, nothing straight was ever made.

If we take this doctrine seriously, we must view the persistence of aporophobia, despite many declarations in favor of the equal dignity of persons and the need to build an inclusive world, as rooted in a human nature marked by an original sin or radical evil that tends to favor the well situated over the less advantaged.

There may also exist a *biological version* of radical evil that could explain why the idealism embodied in politically correct discourses clashes with the lived reality of aporophobia. The answer to this flagrant inconsistency may lie in our brains. Does it play a role in this gulf between words and actions with relation to the poor? The question is far from irrelevant at a moment when neuroscience is helping to clarify the nature of this organ, which weighs some twelve hundred grams, is said to be the most complex structure in the universe, and is the control center of everything we do.

Neuroscience seems to indicate that the conscious mind is not at the center of the brain's actions, and much of what we do, think, and feel eludes our conscious control. Freud already compared the mind to an iceberg, the better part of which was submerged, with the unconscious governing most of our lives; Eagleman entitled his own book about the mind *Incognito: The Secret Lives of the Brain*. Is it here perhaps that the origins of xenophobia and aporophobia lie?

Neuroscience Takes Action

At every point in history, there is some science that takes center stage, inspiring research, projects, and programs at the national and international level. Today this is the case of the neurosciences.[13]

Their long history begins with Hippocrates, and its milestones include Thomas Willis's 1664 treatise *Cerebri Anatome*, John Harlow's article on the brain damage suffered by Phineas Gage, which Antonio Damasio reviewed in *Descartes's Error*, and the findings of Ramón and Cajal.[14] But since the end of the twentieth century, several advances have brought the neurosciences to the forefront: neuroimaging techniques, positron emission tomography, psychopharmaceuticals, brain stimulation techniques, organic implants, and stem cell therapies are all transforming our capacity to understand and change the brain and redefining our understanding of ourselves and the mind-body relationship.[15]

It's true that neuroimaging presents problems. They are not photographs, but maps of which regions of the brain blood is flowing to, and it is not always clear that this is the cause of the phenomenon observed. Interpretation of results often depends on experiment design, and it is common to confuse causes and correlates and fall into the trap of false inferences.[16] Moreover, many results are not open to empirical confirmation.

Still, the field has made undeniable progress across a series of turning points that began with the first conference of the Society of Neuroscientists in the United States in 1971 and continued gathering weight in the nineties, which the United States Congress declared the "Decade of the Brain." In 2013, Barack Obama introduced the *Brain Research through Advancing Innovative Neurotechnologies* (BRAIN), and the European Union inaugurated *The Human Brain Project* (BP), overseen by the neuroscientist Henry Makram.

The immense cost of neuroscience research has led some to suspect that it is a big business promising more than it can deliver, and that it can be applied to marketing or political manipulation as well as to therapy. Recalling Jürgen Habermas's famous essay "Technology and Science as Ideology," one may fear that neuroscience, too, is prone to grading into ideology, and that a critical neuroscience is therefore necessary.[17]

And yet, while adopting necessary precautions, we may learn something from the neurosciences as well as from genetics, molecular biology, anthropology, biology, mathematics, and evolutionary psychology about the bases of human conduct.[18] There may be aspects of the functioning of the human brain that help clarify the personal and social contradictions we have spoken of earlier.

The Chariot Allegory

There exist numerous ways of grasping the nature of the human brain, among them the notion of it as a machine responding automatically to its medium or as an autonomous, active system in constant social interaction. We prefer the second version, which appears the more plausible of the two in light of recent research, and according to it, the brain is in essence an evaluative organ, neither neutral nor alien to values in its functions: to the contrary, it inevitably makes judgments that favor its continued survival.[19]

This evaluative aspect of the brain seems the product of natural selection, because an inability to evaluate stimuli would leave us incapable of learning and remembering. We learn and remember because stimuli reach us in terms of negative and positive values that we keep in mind during the decision-making process. Values play an important role in decision-making at two levels: as a basic biological structure and as a trait of our advanced moral reasoning. In both cases, values are involved in our brain, and it is hence unsurprising that the brain has been described as a narrative organ that weaves its own neuronal tales. Indeed, the brain is less a logical than a narrative processor, and stories attract our attention far more than reasoning does. The idea of the brain as a value-neutral mechanism is insufficient to describe its workings.

And yet, from the time of the early Greeks, we have understood something that is driven home to us each day: in every human being, there are numerous tendencies in conflict that collide rather than harmonize when we are forced to make decisions and act. Plato described this in the chariot allegory, in which two winged horses pull a chariot; Aristotle saw virtue as the attempt to find the right desire among many competing ones; and this idea of competition persists in the history of thought down to Albert Hirschman's description of the birth of capitalism in *The Passions and the Interests*. We must separate the strongest interest, the one that merits attention, from other competing ones.

Eagleman sustains the same in contrast to Marvin Minsky's contentions in *The Society of Mind*. Minsky supposes the mind functions like a machine, a mechanical arrangement of sub-agents, each of which is assigned a task; but, Eagleman objects, Minsky forgets that in society as well as in the brain, these sub-agents compete with one another to control behavior. The parts of a brain are more like rivals than teammates.[20] Their interaction may be explained in a number of ways: as a *double process*, in the view of Evans, in which one system—automatic, implicit, heuristic, intuitive, holistic, reactive, and impulsive—competes with another that is cognitive, systematic, explicit, analytical, rule-based, and reflexive; as a conflict between the Freudian id, ego, and superego; as the encounter between the reptilian brain, the limbic system, and the neocortex that MacLean proposed in 1950. These theories lack the currency they once had, but Eagleman does accept this basic idea of different systems, and he proposes two, one rational and one emotional, which manifest themselves clearly in our decisions with regard to different dilemmas. At any rate, what matters is not the number of systems, but this idea of the brain as comprising rival motivations in conflict that turn decision-making into internal negotiation.

Relevant here is a story Eagleman tells about the actor Mel Gibson. On July 28, 2006, the police pulled him over for speeding and gave him a breathalyzer, and he blew far over the legal limit. The police arrested him for driving under the influence, and Gibson embarked on a diatribe against the Jews. The audio was leaked to the public, and on July 29 the actor released an apology. The public reacted in one of two ways: some felt that the "real Mel Gibson" was the man who uttered the insults (presumably they were drawing on the Greek poet Alcaeus of Mytilene's *en oino aletheia*, later repeated by Pliny in the famous phrase *in vino veritas*). Others said that alcohol and anger could distort a person's thinking. But Eagleman maintains that there is a third possibility: each of us houses different kinds of thoughts that compete with one another even if we are not often conscious of it. And he adds: "I would love it if no one ever thought an anti-Semitic remark, but for better or worse we have little hope of controlling the pathologies of xenophobia that sometimes infect the alien systems. Most of what we call thinking happens well under the surface of cognitive control."[21] *Alien systems* here means those that oversee different tasks in our brain and compete among themselves past our conscious control.

When a remark of this kind that violates the canons of political correctness reaches the social networks and the media, the criticisms fly and the person in question almost always issues a retraction, saying that wasn't what they wished to say or wasn't what they really think. This is naturally an attempt to rescue their reputation—something necessary for life in common, especially in the public eye. But it is important to recognize that such contrary tendencies exist in all of us, that they are engaged in a constant struggle, and that we must know ourselves to reinforce those feelings that are worth having. What are they? Is it possible to control them?

We Are Biologically Xeonophobic

According to Evers and many others, our innate identity, which derives from the species we belong to, predisposes us to develop universal evaluative tendencies that cause us problems throughout our lives as they come into conflict with one another. Our neuronal identity makes us both social and individualistic as tendencies toward self-interest, control, dissociation, selective sympathy, empathy, and xenophobia clash with each other.[22] It is vital to understand what each of these implies.

Self-interest: in essence, the brain is naturally egocentric because it refers all of its experiences to itself. It is a biological self-projection linked to the predisposition to develop basic self-consciousness, which is the precondition for higher orders of consciousness.[23] The child, as it grows, learns to distinguish objects and to distinguish itself from them. Slowly it becomes an object of experience for itself, and by the time it is around one and a half years old, it can distinguish "this thing here" and "me" from "that thing over there." This is a basic evolutionary tendency involved with the biological struggle for survival and the attendant needs to be well fed and safe and to reproduce. This is anterior to the ethical aptitude for distinguishing good and bad.

Basic self-interest, the desire for survival, induces us to *control* our immediate environment and to seek the familiar, the sure, the known. The feeling of security is necessary for healthy development. It is normal that, in our everyday lives, we prefer a controllable environment, even if we do try to incorporate the unknown within the known.

Eagleman contends with reference to xenophobia that a fear of foreigners is absolutely natural. People prefer others who look and talk like them. From the point of view of our culture and our declarations, this aversion is unacceptable, but from the bio-logical one, familiarity brings security and the unusual is uncertain and uncomfortable. That is why we admire people capable of leaving their easy lives behind and setting off on adventures to see unknown lands and peoples.

When we find ourselves in uncomfortable circumstances, we react through the mechanism of *dissociation*, trying to defend ourselves by avoiding integrating unpleasant information. Human beings are *dissociative animals* who invest a great deal of intellectual and emotional energy into distancing themselves from the things they don't like. And this is an important adaptive function for survival.[24]

Self-interest leads us to reject that which disturbs us, whether it be information, events, or persons, while we integrate the things we find acceptable. It is likely here, then, where the roots of phobias lie: in the rejection of the foreign, of that which seems to offer no benefit, disrupts, and is a possible source of problems. *This is the biological root of aporophobia*, that tendency to cast aside what we perceive as unsettling.

Racial and cultural prejudices derive from social emotions that were useful from an evolutionary point of view in detecting differences that might signal risk or danger and toward which escape or aggression was the appropriate response. These reactions were likely suitable in older tribal societies, and even if they are less so now, they remain embedded in our brains.[25]

But possessing a predisposition is not the same as being forced to act in accordance with that sentiment, because the brain possesses enormous plasticity that allows us to modulate it throughout our lives. Then again, there exist other universal evaluative tendencies that we can reinforce to reduce or even eliminate these phobias—for example, the tendency to care for others.

There is an inborn aptitude for the most basic values of look-ing after oneself and one's well-being, but in social animals, this is linked to the care for others one shares ties with. Authors like Patricia Churchland consider this biological tie to lie at the base of morality.[26]

The inclination to care for the young, for friends, and for neighbors is directly or indirectly adaptive because, if it weren't, it wouldn't have been selected for, and the number of those who care for others would have diminished. The neuronal mechanisms of cooperative conduct have likely evolved over 350,000,000 years to optimize us for the care for others, for de-fenseless offspring, and, depending on the empirical condi-tions, for relatives and friends.

The vast majority of neuroethicists believe that these bonds of care extend from relatives to friends to the community, but not to all of humanity. Evolution has clearly selected for dis-criminating bonds of care.[27] For this reason, we can speak of another universal tendency, that of *selective sympathy*, which is extended to others in relation to their closeness in biological terms: facial recognition, ingroup and outgroup distinctions, culture, ideology, and so on. Selective sympathy promotes group cooperation and discerning who is *us* and who is *them*.[28] And this differentiation leads to inevitable conflicts when self-interest clashes with cooperation.

Sympathy requires empathy, the capacity to grasp the feel-ings of others, putting ourselves imaginatively in their place, reconstructing their experience in our imagination, knowing their joy, sorrow, pleasure, and pain. According to some inter-pretations, empathy has its origins in mirror neurons and exists thanks to interior simulations.[29] But empathy is not yet sympa-thy, because it is possible to grasp the affective state of another without yielding to it. The torturer is highly *empathetic* with his victim, understanding what torments will hurt most, but his approach is *dissociative*, so that this pain doesn't affect him.

Sympathy, on the other hand, leads the person who feels it to be affected by the other's situation—it opens us to the pain of others.[30] These capacities presuppose complex cognitive functions touching on biological and cultural values. And sympathy, being selective, bringing us closer to those near us but not to strangers, makes us naturally *empathetically xenophobic*.[31]

It therefore follows that any attempt at building social structures that modulate sympathetic identification must attend to this biological challenge as well as cultural, political, and social challenges. This is not something new: our brain has a history that has led us here.

A Brief History of the Xenophobic Brain

Though much of this history is speculative because we lack direct empirical evidence of it, in neuroethics it is a truism that our brains evince codes of conduct selected through evolution. At the origin of social relations, people lived together in small groups of no more than 130 racially homogenous people sharing the same customs. The codes that were incorporated into the brain were fundamentally emotional and were necessary to survive and encourage mutual aid, social cohesion, and suspicion toward strangers.[32] This is the beginning of the story of the xenophobic brain, acquired through long evolution, which some consider the basis of the most primitive behavioral codes.[33]

These conclusions derive, among other things, from studies showing how brains react when asked to resolve moral dilemmas affecting those close to the subject or others who are further away in space or emotionally—personal versus impersonal dilemmas.[34] Physical proximity activates deep emotional-moral survival codes, while its absence activates colder cognitive codes distant from the immediate need for survival.

Neuroimaging techniques allow us to observe heightened activity in the areas that play crucial roles in emotional processing, in the circuit linking the frontal lobe to the limbic system, in personal moral situations. Greene concludes that when subjects form idiosyncratic judgments, there is greater activation of the dorsolateral prefrontal cortex, which is implicated in planning and reasoning. Judgments about personal moral dilemmas thus seem to demand greater activity in the parts of the brain associated with emotion and social cognition.

This is why we are personally affected by the situation of those close to us and not with those we do not know: from the evolutionary perspective, the neuronal structures that associate the instincts with the emotions were selected because helping those in our immediate surroundings is immediately beneficial. This is the key to group altruism, which brought human beings close to those they needed to survive, those familiar to them, those they feel safest with. Strangers, people who are different, represent a danger in the biological sense. Hence xenophobia is biologically rooted. Is aporophobia as well?

Aporophobia: The Excluded

Evolutionary anthropology and neuroethics refer often to Darwin's difficulties in establishing a basis for altruism in *On the Origin of Species*. Darwin found natural selection a less than adequate basis for explaining why those who triumph in the struggle for existence are not the selfish, but rather the altruists, those who devote part of their energies to the adaptation of others. In principle, natural selection ought to favor those who do not go to war and take advantage of the fact that others do, while those who die in war defending the group ought not to be able to reproduce. How is the persistence of altruists to be explained? Altruism seems to confer benefits on its receiver and costs on the person who engages in it, because it represents for the latter a diminished investment in his own adaptation, and natural selection should eventually eliminate those who reduce their own reproductive value in favor of others.

Darwin's response was to resort to the idea of group selection. The small groups human beings lived in for much of their evolution required the solidarity of their members to survive. Altruistic conduct conferred no benefits on the individuals within a group, but did allow for selection among groups, so that those most tightly bound survived better in the struggle for life. In Darwin's words:

> It must not be forgotten that although a high standard of morality gives but a slight or no advantage to each individual man and his children over the other men of the same tribe, yet that an increase in the number of well-endowed men and an advancement in the standard of morality will certainly give an immense advantage to one tribe over another. A tribe including many members who, from possessing in a high degree the spirit of patriotism, fidelity, obedience, courage, and sympathy, were always ready to aid one another, and to sacrifice themselves for the common good, would be victorious over most other tribes; and this would be natural selection.[35]

Darwin's explanation is an attractive one for grasping why altruistic individuals are motivated by group pressure. Group survival demands individual sacrifice for the love of the group as well as for self-interest, but ingroup altruism is inevitably xenophobic, excluding those marked as *other*.

But the idea that exclusion is inevitable, that selective sympathy for ingroup members obviates compassion for others, seems refuted by instances of altruism shown to people outside the group. And so the hypothesis that group selection explains altruism is flawed, and has been succeeded by a broad range of contending theories from Dawkins's selfish gene to Hamilton's genetic altruism, which states that individual altruism is an attempt to protect one's genes.[36] Hamilton offers an update of the golden rule present in all secular and religious moralities with his phrase: "Do unto others to the degree to which they share your genes."[37]

But this, too, is insufficient to explain biological altruism, because some actions costly to individuals benefit others to whom they are not related. Hence we must affirm that all human beings, and perhaps some animals, are capable of reciprocation: that there are altruistic actions that cannot be explained by ingroup dynamics, but only by the *expectation of reciprocity*.

And this is one of the keys for understanding human conduct: human beings are predisposed to give so long as the expectation exists of receiving something in return—predisposed to cooperation as a mode of surviving and thriving more intelligent than conflict-seeking.

The notion that human beings are guided by maximizing rationality, seeking the greatest benefit at any cost, has been discredited. It is more rational to seek cooperation than conflict, to create allies rather than seek adversaries. This is why prudent individuals and organizations work cooperatively, running their enterprises in a cooperative manner and often opting for the second- or third-best option, which serves all, rather than seeking maximum profit at any cost. Working in common always leads to positive outcomes and generates bonds of cooperation that are highly desirable in the medium and long term.

People are thus coming to realize that the figure of *homo economicus* as a profit-maximizing creature must be replaced with that of *homo reciprocans*, a being capable of giving and receiving, of cooperating, of rational conduct—and that this is the fruit of instincts and emotions and not just of utility-maximizing calculations.[38] The understanding that a back-and-forth of giving and receiving is beneficial for groups and individuals has crystallized it into the norms of indirect reciprocity that form the bedrock of the contractual societies we live in, ruled over by a principle of exchange. Every action supposes a response, and reciprocation is the basis of cooperation, but benefits may in many cases accrue to third parties.

This is what Kropotkin refers to in his classic of anarchism, *Mutual Aid: A Factor of Evolution*, which documents the superiority of mutual aid to competition in the struggle for survival. Kant likewise realized this decades before in his article "Perpetual Peace," in which he writes that a race of devils, so long as they were intelligent, would prefer to organize into a state protected by laws to living in a lawless state in which life, property, and the freedom to determine their future were not secured.[39]

And so there are biological predispositions to selfishness and to cooperation, and the idea of the purely selfish individual is an ideological fiction. Adaptive principles have given rise to a contractualist brain that drives us neither to look for the greatest good for the greatest number nor to promote the already prosperous, but to seal a pact of mutual aid with all those we need to survive and thrive.

What then, is to be said of that evaluative tendency on the part of our species that leads us to shove away that which is unsettling, which yields no benefit—of our nature as *dissociative animals* ever ready to bracket off problematic people and situations, those alienated from the infinite process of exchange, who seem in no way to contribute to our survival and well-being? Racism and xenophobia exist. Nepotism and amoral familism exist. A kind of rustic communitarianism exists that reinforces the symbols and identity of the group in ways reminiscent of hunter-gatherer times. However much judicious people and institutions have learned the advantages of cooperation over conflictive profit maximization, it remains true that in a contractualist and cooperative society based on exchange, the *radical stranger* who is excluded from this interplay is pushed aside as one who offers no possible return benefit. This person is, in social terms, poor, and taking account of him implies the loss of biological and social adaptive capacity, as only the well situated help us to survive and thrive.

Who are these powerless people? They may be the handicapped, the mentally ill, the undocumented, castoffs, those without influential friends, those who cannot offer favors, jobs, positions, money, votes, electoral support, honors, and the prerogatives that stoke the vanity of others.

The expectation of exchange is the biological and social environment in which aporophobia grows. And these need not be strangers in the pure sense; indeed, it is often worse if they are close to us and can cause us problems, and when they are part of our own family, they may be treated like a source of shame that must be concealed.

The good news is our brain has enormous plasticity and may be influenced socially, even before we are born.[40] Nature and nurture influence one another, and so the structure of our brain is biosocial, with learning and experience mingled with our genetics.[41] Essential, then, are formal and informal education, the decisions taken in the course of a life, and the creation of institutions and organizations that demand the recognition of the powerless.

To make real the shared dream that began this chapter, neither selfishness nor the desire for cooperation are sufficient. We
must go beyond them to the reciprocal recognition of dignity
and to compassion, breaking barriers and extending them uni-
versally.[42] This is not written in our genes or inscribed in our
brains, but it has come down to us through cultural traditions
that have made of it the human experience par excellence.

Chapter 5

Conscience and Reputation

A bad conscience is easier to cope with than a bad reputation.

—FRIEDRICH NIETZSCHE, *THE GAY SCIENCE*

The Need to Educate the Conscience

The cognitive and social bases of aporophobia can be modified, and the best way to do so is through education, understood in the broader sense, and the formation of economic, political, and social institutions capable of encouraging respect for the equal dignity of all people. But these avenues are not open without that which has traditionally been called *moral conscience*, taking the reins of one's own life and striving toward one's own goals rather than in thrall to external pressures.

True, more recently some have proposed opting for a third, rather novel option—moral bioenhancement, which we will examine in the following chapter. But even if we consider improving moral motivation through existing means such as pharmaceuticals, there must exist prior to this a personal conscience capable of freely choosing these remedies—they cannot be imposed in an authoritarian manner. Only freedom can be a path toward freedom.

The other side of the coin of conscience is that account society takes of our actions, which is known as reputation. The good or bad reputation of people, companies, organizations, and institutions is a powerful instrument society can use to incentivize certain actions and inhibit others, to reinforce prosocial conduct or punish its opposite. It is thus necessary to keep in mind the force of reputation while also strengthening the conscience so that it knows how to discern and act without social imperatives. Otherwise, we will only eschew those phobias proscribed by the larger society, continuing to practice those deemed acceptable.

The Ring of Gyges

At the beginning of his novel *The Good Conscience,* Carlos Fuentes repeats a phrase that he attributes to Emmanuel Mounier.[1] In fact, the phrase comes from Nietzsche, and we quote it at the beginning of this chapter. Fuentes repeats it in French: "On s'arrange mieux de sa mauvaise conscience que de sa mauvaise reputation."[2] This principle is seen in all its implications in the development of the book.

The author is referring here to two dimensions of the human world, which we might call internal and external. Conscience would represent the internal world; reputation would refer to the way society evaluates a person's actions. There is a type of conscience and of reputation that merits the description *moral,* inquiring as to whether they might not coincide and whether it indeed makes sense to speak of this internal-external distinction. It may be that moral conscience is nothing but the internalization on the part of subjects of the rules of an actually existing society or an ideal society in which the subject would wish to reside.

This clashes with the famous tale of Gyges's ring that appears in Book II of Plato's *Republic*, which suggests that people's behavior is determined entirely by the exterior. The story appears in a dialogue on justice conducted by Glaucon, Adeimanthus, Thrasymachus, and Socrates. Glaucon relates that a pastor found a ring that made its wearer invisible when he turned it. He uses it to seduce the Queen of Lydia, kill the king, and take over the kingdom. Glaucon makes a striking point: if there were two such rings, and one was given to a just man and the other to an unjust one, their behavior would not differ, because "no one is just of his own will but only from constraint, in the belief that justice is not his personal good, inasmuch as every man, when he supposes himself to have the power to do wrong, does wrong."[3] Justice is done not because it is good in itself, but because one lacks the power to commit injustice.

Glaucon is playing the devil's advocate. He is sure that justice is good in itself and not because of the consequences it may give rise to, and that injustice is to be rejected as such; but with his story, he hopes to provoke Socrates to speak decisively on the behalf of justice. Glaucon feels the vulgar position is that injustice is more advantageous personally than justice, and that it is wise to appear to act justly from fear of the loss of reputation or other forms of social reprimand. He imagines Socrates will offer decisive arguments to topple these commonplaces.

Putting aside Plato's text, is it possible that the vulgar position is right? Is what we have called moral conscience, which should be integral to our idea of justice, a mere calculation as to how far one may go seeking to benefit oneself without provoking opprobrium?

The question of the nature of moral conscience has persisted throughout the history of philosophy, from the Pythagoreans, Socrates, Plato, Aristotle, the Stoics and Epicureans, the medieval doctors, the Enlightenment philosophes, and Hegel, down through the school of suspicion, which questioned the centrality of conscience, to Heidegger, Lévinas, and Jonas, who restored its prominence, and in the twenty-first century, it remains a subject of widespread reflection. But the triumph of moral naturalism increasingly promotes an understanding of conscience, not as an inner *daimon* in the Socratic sense, but as a *prudential calculation related to reputation.*

The question is an essential one. In social life, moral conscience is indispensable in modern societies that recognize the freedom of conscience, conscientious objection, conscience clauses, and civil disobedience. Responsibility, the obligation to compel oneself, forms much of the core of moral life. How can we criticize corruption, deceit, or hypocrisy if the conscience consists of the fear of the loss of reputation and nothing more? How can we educate moral subjects, which are the foundation of a democratic society, if the task of creating an independent conscience is futile?

Moll's characterization of morality, widely recognized in the social sciences, is interesting here. A specialist in moral emotions, he describes them as "linked to the interest either of society as a whole, or at least of persons other than the judge or agent."[4] The tendency to align morality with conduct that suppresses selfishness and contributes to solidarity is common, epitomized in that phrase of Durkheim's that Jonathan Haidt refers to, stressing that morality is everything that is the source of solidarity and forces man to regulate his actions through something other than selfishness.[5] Haidt expands upon this conception, stating that "moral systems are interlocking sets of values, virtues, norms, practices, identities, institutions, technologies, and evolved psychological mechanisms that work together to suppress or regulate self-interest and make cooperative societies possible."[6]

Morality consists, then, of the sum of values, principles, and customs that restrain selfishness and reinforce cooperation and solidarity, first among human beings of a polity, and eventually among mankind as a whole. Coexistence between radically selfish beings would be impossible; morality is thus a product of evolutionary pressures that have given rise to social-cognitive and emotional mechanisms that were already present in our ancestors and help shape the human forms of experience. The evolution of the frontal cortex is closely related to the emergence of morality. How did this evolution occur?

The Biological Evolution of the Moral Conscience

The long history of the study of moral conscience in Western philosophy is generally thought to begin with Socrates. It may appear that it has been a preoccupation, in the main, of non-naturalists, that is to say, authors whose reflections have aimed beyond sensory experience toward an abstract realm that is the domain of universal concepts and values not rooted in biology.[7] But this is not the case, as we can see in the preeminently naturalist example of Charles Darwin, who affirms:

> I fully subscribe to the judgment of those writers who maintain that of all the differences between man and the lower animals, the moral sense or conscience is by far the most important. This sense, as Mackintosh remarks, "has a rightful supremacy over every other principle of human action."[8]

According to Darwin, the moral conscience is not an insignificant dimension of human life, but the most important distinction between man and animal; he insists on this repeatedly throughout his work. There do exist common traits between human beings and such animals as chimpanzees that might be described as "proto-moral" or, in De Waal's term, the *building blocks* of morality, including reciprocity, consolation, aversion to inequality, empathy, and the mutual reinforcement of rules of conduct.[9] There is debate about the extent to which animals truly possess these traits, but regardless, they are not fully capable of developing moral sense or conscience, which is, according to Darwin:

> ultimately a highly complex sentiment, having its first origin in the social instincts, largely guided by the approbation of our fellow-men, ruled by reason, self-interest, and in later times by deep religious feelings, confirmed by instruction and habit, all combined, constitute our moral sense or conscience.[10]

The *origin* of moral conscience lies in human's social instinct, which permits the growth of a series of characteristics nonhuman animals lack.[11] This idea of the *social origin* of conscience is commonplace when discussing its biological origins, and this is perhaps why its personal aspect is often forgotten and the moral and the social come to be identified with one another.

The evolutionary appearance of moral conscience seems linked to the "mystery of biological altruism."[12] How does the hypothesis of natural selection explain the persistence of altruism across time? Darwin proposed group selection as a possible cause: altruistic conduct affords benefits not to individuals within groups, but to groups in competition with others, with solidary groups proving fitter in the struggle for survival.[13] This, however, does not explain the persistence of altruistic individuals alongside free riders who seek to minimize risks. For this, we need a closer examination of the moral conscience.

The Feeling of Shame and Moralist Aggression

The most convincing response is that groups have protected themselves throughout their evolution by punishing free riders through physical elimination, ostracism, or shame, destroying their reputation. This is known as social selection.

In 1971, Robert Trivers defined "moralistic aggression" as a selective force for enforcing norms among hunter-gatherers. This form of coercion remains ever-present in our societies.[14] It led to a banishment of free riders in hunter-gatherer societies, giving them few chances to reproduce, while altruists, more appreciated by their communities, had proportionally more such opportunities.[15] For this system to work, it was necessary for individuals to acquire a group of traits essential for the development of moral conscience. Taken as a whole, these are what Alexander calls "indirect reciprocity." They represent the capacity to intuit the intentions of others, to detect those who are intentionally violating group norms, to punish infractors even if this is difficult, and to delay gratification.[16]

For moral conscience to emerge, it is necessary that there exist *the awareness of laws governing the group, of the physical or psychological punishment infringing upon them that may incur, and of the possibility of scorn*, of the shame that may succeed a loss of reputation within the group. The last of these is seen as essential to survival. In his time, Darwin wrote to colonial administrators and missionaries asking them whether the indigenous peoples of Asia and Africa blushed, and concluded that all human beings do, and that the ability to do so is unique to them. It thus appears that shame reactions are innate rather than cultural.[17]

The significance of the *feeling of shame and the longing for reputation* among individuals and groups leads one to speculate upon the cultural value of gossip as an essential step in human moral evolution. Presumably, hunter-gatherers shared critical information about violators of group norms while themselves acting in an altruistic way to maintain their own reputations. Concern for praise and fear of reproach would then be the most important stimuli for the development of social virtues and the feeling of sympathy that grounds them.[18] Sympathy—the capacity for understanding the suffering and joy of others—is required for compassion and solidarity, but it also gives rise to mutual dependence, because we care about our reputations—about the vision these people have of us.[19]

The Natural Garden of Eden

This naturally brings to mind the Book of Genesis and Adam and Eve's shame at the realization that they were nude when they violated the divine commandment. Awareness of the law and shame at violating it seem to lie at the origin of our understanding of good and evil. There are biblical and naturalist versions of the Eden parable: in the first, the mandate is divine, in the second it is biological.[20]

Bodily shame in Genesis can be seen as an expression of the sense of guilt present in societies that placed great stress on formalities surrounding sexual relations. But it may also express the shame one feels at being discovered violating norms, at being exposed to public reproof, with the attendant loss of reputation. The expulsion from Eden may be a metaphor for the fatigue of work and the pains of childbirth, but also for the deep spiritual suffering of recognizing oneself as a lawbreaker. The same is true of Cain, who was punished for his crime and exiled to the Land of Nod, east of Eden.

Some intellectuals today see social shame as a mechanism for putting an end to corruption and malpractice, but it is a double-edged sword: anyone can use it, not only those who are right and just, and it follows the norms of the group, which are not always right and just. It can be turned on the weak, on those who offer no benefit and who cannot avenge themselves, and can thus become just another instrument by which the powerful oppress others. We must therefore develop our powers of discernment and critical capacities to maintain awareness of who the weak parties are in each situation.

What Is the Voice of Conscience?

Of the extant explanations of what moral conscience is, the evolutionary perspective has offered two versions of particular interest. One conceives it as a strategic inner voice instructing us as to the best way to pursue our interests without provoking the ire of the group. According to this version, human beings are selfish and must balance out their pursuit of their own interests without losing their reputation and their wealth. As Alexander writes, moral conscience in this view is the "still small voice that tells us how far we can go in serving our own interests without incurring intolerable risks."[21]

We may also interpret it as less strategic, but equally adaptive, as a tendency to identify with the values of one's own community, with the rules of the group, connecting with them emotionally in such a way that we feel pride when we uphold them and shame when we do not.[22] This identification favors group integration, the feeling and knowledge of acceptance, which is one of the basic human needs in Abraham Maslow's famous pyramid.

Here, neurobiology's relationship to consciousness consists in the pain we feel at rejection and the pleasure of belonging to a group and imitating those we admire.[23] Different areas of the brain have evolved to endow us with our moral faculty, which is a sense of right and wrong, a capacity to blush and feel shame, a feeling of empathy, an awareness that we can be punished, a consciousness of our limits and how close to them we can come, of our reputation and of the fact that a good one is beneficial. Conscience helps us make decisions to maintain our reputation and appear to be valuable people, and this is the source of our self-esteem, one of the goods that no person would want to do without.[24]

But what of the case of the infractor who goes undiscovered, has no cause for shame, and loses none of his reputation? Here we are taken back to the tale of Gyges's ring. According to Glaucon, the just and unjust man will kill, rob, and rape alike, because the ring frees them from the conditions that oblige them to be just in order to survive. The just man, in this account, is so because he lacks sufficient power to commit injustice. We accept justice because we are weak; otherwise, we would not. Socrates's response—"He who acts in such a way is not a just man"—may be attractive, but it seems dubious in light of the biological account of the origins of moral conscience, according to which *people attend to the call of conscience because their behavior is visible.* In this sense, the role of reputation is indispensable.

The Force of Reputation

In their article "Shrewd Investments," evolutionary mathematicians Nowak and Sigmund tell the story of an old academic who attends the funerals of his colleagues because otherwise, they won't attend his.[25] For them, this anecdote reveals a basic human trait: no matter what we do, we expect some kind of recompense. Reciprocation is the basis of cooperation. The old professor wasn't wrong to expect his colleagues to attend his funeral to the extent that he trusted in indirect reciprocity, which demands restitution not from the beneficiaries of one's own altruism, but from third parties. Alexander considers this the "basis of all systems of morality."[26]

But for this altruism to be realized, the expectation of benefits must exceed perceived costs,[27] and while this can be assured with a measure of probability between altruist and beneficiary, the bonds between giver and receiver are broken in indirect reciprocity, and the indirect path to recompense may be taken advantage of by free riders and spongers off of the benefits of a contractualist society.

The reputation of a person, company, organization, professional, or political group forms the bond between the act of giving and the expectation of receiving, and this inspires confidence on the part of those who fulfill their obligations that compensation will arrive in due time. This may be a personal benefit or one that accrues to others and keeps the chains of exchange alive and thriving. This is the economy of the gift described by Marcel Mauss, and it is present in any contractual economy: if indirect reciprocity functions, it is thanks to the mechanism of reputation and status that extends across society.

It is from this perspective that Nowak and Sigmund take as the symbol of moral pressure the ever-vigilant eye in the sky that has so often represented an omnipresent god, seeing conscience as an internalization of our way of being with others. This may be the ultimate meaning of philanthropy on the part of individuals and organizations, as their donations are usually known to the public. Despite the evangelical mandate to keep them secret, with the right hand unaware what the left is doing, word does get out, and it is usually a boon to marketing.

In recent years, studies have shown that prosocial conduct is linked to the desire for a good reputation.[28] In economic ex-

periments, especially, individuals act egotistically when anonymity is guaranteed, while they exhibit prosocial tendencies
in a less anonymous setting—even when there are photos or
drawings as opposed to real observers.[29]

And so Nietzsche was right to affirm that outside of those
exceptional cases that always exist, people, companies, political
parties, and their leaders care a great deal more what others
think about them than what they think about themselves. Perhaps because, as Machiavelli reminded the prince who he felt
was tasked with achieving power and salvaging the republic,
"All see what you appear to be, few feel what you are." The world
of appearances is the one that is attractive to the will and per-
suades or dissuades, while what a person really is remains a
mystery of individuals' conscience.

Hence, the intelligent person labors after a good reputation.
The media constantly present the citizens' opinions of their political leaders, with the presumption that their reputation will
influence the number of votes they receive; companies publish
corporate responsibility statements that they offer to potential
clients, other companies, and politicians, in the understanding
that an ethical image is key to good business.

This has perhaps always been true, but it is much more so in
the internet era, when visibility has multiplied exponentially
and reputations are built on *likes* and *dislikes* that determine the
fate of hotels, articles, books, and travel agencies. Creating or
destroying a reputation isn't difficult so long as one is smart
enough to mobilize people's emotions in a certain direction,
with simple, schematic messages that appeal to the sentiments
of the majority. Far more than the era of Machiavelli, Nietzsche,
or Mounier, ours is an era of reputations, where knowing how
to manipulate emotions is essential to success.

Educating for Autonomy and Compassion

Those studies that reflect the importance of social pressure on individual conduct and the evolutionary process offer interesting conclusions about how to orient personal and community action. If we act in a more prosocial manner when we feel under observation, we should send a clear message that our societies reject aporophobic conduct and support actions aimed at empowering the poor; that we favor inclusive over exclusive actions; that we prefer to take in and not reject those who appear to have nothing to offer in return; that we agree with Adam Smith that the objects of contempt should be vice and stupidity rather than poverty. This must be borne in mind in education, business, and politics.

If these are the norms of our society, our children will incorporate them passively, because the cultural and social world begins to leave its mark on them even before they are born. The ethical rules of a community, which are linked to the symbolic representation of its character, have such an effect on the young that we ought not to speak of pure biological evolution, but rather of biocultural evolution.

But at this point, we have strayed far from the Socratic notion of the conscience as an inner voice that reminds us of what is just and urges us to act with justice irrespective of the consequences. A society's norms are not always rationally valid, and those who choose justice at the expense of their reputation or violate the biological and social mandate to conform to unjust rules should not be morally disqualified. Is there not within the moral conscience an *unconditional obligation* that stands above concern for reputation?

Conscience may function within a framework of pure selfishness, calculating the degree to which individual benefit may be sought without breaking societal norms; it may likewise adapt to the norms of a society to live within it comfortably; but these two ways of describing conscience are inadequate, leaving aside many important aspects of human life.

Figures such as Socrates or Antigone epitomize the idea of the contradiction between the dictates of conscience and the rules of society, and their example persists in the long history of martyrs, conscientious objectors, civil disobedience, and resistance movements. Sometimes people oppose a society's laws to obey the law of God; other times, they follow a higher law to which they believe humanity is consigned; other times, they follow their own law according to an ethics of authenticity. Whoever objects to the laws of a given society can be said to do so with another real or ideal society in mind that serves as a model; regardless, this person accepts the laws he follows not because doing so enables him to live in peace; indeed, he sacrifices his comfort for the sake of a creed he considers more proper.

The evolutionary interpretation of the moral conscience also fails to explain the emergence of moral creators, moral innovators, who have offered paths superior to, and at times contrary to, the laws of society. They break with the norms of closed systems of morals and offer extraordinary alternatives.[30] Buddha or Jesus, to take two examples, are innovators in this sense, and Darwin would recognize as much of the latter:

> To do good in return for evil, to love your enemy, is a height of morality to which it may be doubted whether the social instincts would, by themselves, have ever led us. It is necessary that these instincts, together with sympathy, should have been highly cultivated and extended by the aid of reason, instruction, and the love or fear of God, before any such golden rule would ever be thought of and obeyed.[31]

Morality is generally linked to the kinds of customs and norms that demand the suppression of selfishness and concern themselves with other human beings or with the collective. But there is another set of duties traditionally called duties to oneself that oblige a subject to respect himself and not worry solely over others. An awareness of these duties, which appear in traditional works of morality, is born, according to Darwin, with civilization itself. Civilized societies, unlike barbaric ones, are concerned with their self-image.[32]

Here, there is an interesting point of coincidence between two different authors, Darwin and Kant, because Kant, too, considers an awareness of duties toward oneself inseparable from moral life. In his Doctrine of Virtue in *The Metaphysics of Morals*, Kant distinguishes between the duties man has toward himself and those he has toward others, and he begins his analysis with the first, understanding that the key to all morality is *self-obligation*. Duty cannot consist merely in the fulfillment of obligations toward others; it is, in the first place, fulfilling obligations to oneself, and the knowledge that one is obliged to fulfill obligations toward others derives from this obligation of the self.[33]

The character of moral obligation consists in transcending the demands of any other form of social coercion: we may be biologically programmed to follow group norms to avoid reproach, punishment, and the loss of reputation, and reason may remind us of this, but all this would vanish for the unjust person who slips on Gyges's ring; while a being endowed with moral rationality is capable of obliging itself, for which reason there exists a specific moral world that unconditionally orders us to adopt rules when we consider them just and to dismiss them when we consider them just, irrespective of the group.

This human capacity bears the name "autonomy" or "moral freedom." The motive for following the laws of freedom is not pragmatic, but is rather the respect for the dignity of beings that are valuable in themselves because they are free.

Internal obligation, which does not proceed from group pressure, has been explained throughout history by the presence of a natural law within the conscience, which some metaphysicians have described as the law of God, of humanity, of the imperative to be what you are. In all cases, this is an inner force bound not to the need for survival but to the desire to live *well*, in accordance with one's own conscience. The Stoics called this "living in accordance with nature," religious philosophers have called it "living according to the law of God," Kantians "living in accord with the law of reason," and authenticity ethics call it living in accord with the incorruptible depths of oneself.

Without internal obligation, people are left at the mercy of social pressure, jostling for reputation, group norms, which do not always favor inclusion over exclusion or acceptance over rejection. They are prone to selfish calculation or accommodationism, which may be necessary to survive and prosper, but which are insufficient to living a full life. Educating for autonomy, to forge a conscience through dialogue and argumentation, one that will not buckle to social pressure when it is arbitrary rather than reasoned, is necessary for the survival of moral life.[34]

A bad reputation may be a burden, with horrible consequences for our self-esteem and for our ability to carry through our desires and aspirations. A good or bad conscience, on the other hand, remains inside us. Conscience seems something "all too neglected," as Saint-Éxupery's little prince says. Ours is a time of reputation and not of conscience.

And yet much of public life is based on the supposition that we struggle to abide by a guilty conscience. Politicians appeal to their conscience and honor when they swear to uphold their obligations—in Spain they take this oath before the Constitution. It's perfectly logical, in a pluralistic society, that the nonbeliever swear on something other than a sacred book. But it's no less logical to suppose that such a person believes in his conscience and values it to such a degree that he is unwilling to betray it at any cost. To avoid citizens lying in court, Kant recommends in *The Metaphysics of Morals* the preservation of faith in a god capable of punishing perjurers; but if, in our time, the final guarantor of conscience is personal, we must suppose that it is something we esteem highly.

The appeal to conscience naturally does not exempt a society from creating laws, ideally clear and precise ones based on transparency, accountability, and responsibility. Accountability before the citizenry is proper to a democratic society in which the people are said to be the governors. Still, the question remains open: Who governs the governors?

Enlightened parties who in principle refuse any judge apart from their own conscience are a danger; even more so are fanatics who kill without compassion in thrall to the faith held by their group. Thus, the personal conscience must be formed through dialogue, never through monologue, and not even through dialogue with proximate groups like the family, the ethnic group, even the nation. We are human beings, and nothing human should be alien to us—dialogue must take into account those near to and far from us in space and time.

Contractual relations are not the only form of bond between human beings—we do not live by giving and receiving alone. There is also an involuntary bond between human beings, one that exists a priori and that we may break or reinforce. Each person is what he is because he is recognized as a person; reciprocal recognition constitutes a bond, a *ligatio*, with the two members of an encounter. There are no isolated individuals, only people in relation to one another.

Hence, the worst punishment that can be imposed is condemnation to invisibility, ignoring the existence of the other, rejection, contempt. Reciprocal recognition is what constitutes our human essence, which makes us capable of living in the compassionate recognition that forms the base of an inclusive society.

Discovering this tie, this *ligatio* of mutual belonging, gives rise to those obligations, like that of respecting others' dignity, which are the natural domain of justice. Further, they open the way to the warmth of gratitude.

Chapter 6

Moral Bioenhancement

The Problem of Moral Motivation

Traditionally, personal and social conscience have been shaped by education. Education is also, as we have noted, a way of overcoming the social pathologies normally marked by the suffix "phobia." The purpose here is to bring our actions in line with our declarations, overcoming weaknesses in our personal and social conscience. A key factor in this process of enhancement or improvement is motivation.

A moral motivation sufficient to promote universalist norms that protect all persons and not merely those capable of offering advantages to us is scarce enough that we have failed to eliminate from our daily lives scorn for those groups who cannot do so. Aporophobia throbs in this scorn, and is embodied in xenophobia, racism, homophobia, misogyny, and aversion to other religions or ideologies.

It is likewise difficult to avoid such moral pathologies as corruption, perversion of justice, bribery, and favoring oneself and one's group over the common good, in politics and business as well as in other organizations and institutions. The rector of a Spanish university remarked that his job required attending to the vanity of five hundred powerful professors willing to re-scind their support if they did not receive privileges and recognition from those who oversaw the university. In systems of this kind, injustice is obviously inevitable.

Education is a system for motivating sentiments opposed to the neglect of the less fortunate, and a knowledge of the functioning of the brain may be helpful here. Such books as María José Codina's *Neuroeducation in Cordial Virtues* move in this direction. Yet every day we see evidence that education is insufficient. Not because the laws are better or worse or the curricula more or less adequate, but because at present, society does not instill in its members respect for dignity or compassion.

Rarely or never do the parents of a bully admit that he is harming his weaker companions. Rarely or never do parents admit that their children have failed a subject because they didn't study. If they get a bit of power, they will stand up to the teacher and destroy his life if needed as long as their child comes out smelling like roses. They will turn to other teachers, the media, counselors, will send endless conspiratorially minded WhatsApp messages, will do anything they can to tarnish the reputation of the teacher who has dared reveal to their child the natural consequences of not studying. And often they will be successful, because they have votes and relationships and friendships and those things are more compelling incentives for politicians than justice and honor. The law is impotent before this kind of behavior, and powerful consumers manipulate it at their will. The *aporoi* on the other hand have no card to play here. For this reason, some authors in recent years have proposed that education's failure to improve morality among the people suggests the need to turn to more expedient means that technology has now put in our hands: namely, moral bioenhancement.

The New Frankenstein

In recent years, advances in the biomedical sciences have generated new methods for improving human biology.[1] Biomedical
techniques developed through the examination of pathologies
are routinely employed to maintain or restore health, but they
may also be used to change the characteristics of people deemed
healthy or improve those considered normal.

Such possibilities bring to light one ethical dilemma in particular: Are enhancement procedures ethically acceptable, or
only therapeutic ones? And if they are, then are we morally
obliged to improve "normal" cognitive or physical capacities
or memory or attention skills if the possibility exists?[2] If we
accept Amartya Sen's contentions, improving human beings'
capacities would be a form of empowering them. And if we
take seriously the Kantian affirmation that the human being
is the positive and negative end of our actions, improving
people's capacities would be a way of taking man as a positive
end in scientific interventions.

This issue of enhancement has become an essential theme in
bio- and especially neuroethics as they attempt to decide what
kinds of interventions are acceptable or even obligatory, and
whether we must necessarily use all the means in our grasp, up
to and including biotechnology, to improve human capabilities,
as a contemporary Frankenstein would wish to.

William Safire referred to these difficulties at a groundbreak-
ing conference in 2002, when he claimed that neuroethics had
been founded two centuries before in 1816 at a Villa Diodati on
the outskirts of Geneva.[3] This is where Lord Byron, Percy Shelley, John Polidori, and Mary Shelley gathered during a storm
and decided to amuse themselves by writing a horror story
somehow related to man's perfectibility. This was the origin of

Polidori's *The Vampire*, but the one that soon became famous was Mary Shelley's *Frankenstein*. Neuroethics, Safire affirmed, was born of the Promethean longing to improve human beings' mental and physical capacities until they reached perfection.

Is this true? Are the biomedical sciences aiming for a contemporary version of Frankenstein's monster?

Transhumanists and Bioconservatives

To reply, we must ask what we mean by enhancement. Alan Buchanan describes it as a "deliberate intervention, applying biomedical science, which aims to improve an existing capacity that most or all human beings typically have, or to create a new capacity, by acting directly on the body or brain."[4] Julian Savulescu prefers the following definition: "X is an enhancement for A if X makes it more probable that A will live a better life in circumstances C, which are a group of natural and social circumstances."[5]

The first raises the difficulty of deciding what are the typical capacities most human beings have, while the second is broadly utilitarian: whether or not a capacity is normal is irrelevant, what matters is whether improving it allows one to live better.

In their introduction to the book *Human Enhancement*, the authors, Savulescu and Bostrom, highlight two positions with regard to the ethics of bioenhancement as opposed to mere therapeutic interventions or treatments: the transhumanist and the bioconservative.[6] They recognize themselves as transhumanists, to the point that Nick Bostrom founded the World Transhumanist Association in 1998 with David Pearce for the purpose of creating an organization base for all transhumanist groups. The two men are also the authors of the Transhumanist

Declaration and founders of the *Journal of Transhumanism*, which would later change its name to the *Journal of Evolution and Technology*.[7]

To define transhumanism, it is useful to turn to the biologist and first director general of the UN, Julian Huxley, brother of Aldous Huxley. In *New Bottles for New Wine*, he writes: "The human species can, if it wishes, transcend itself—not just sporadically, an individual here in one way, an individual there in another way, but in its entirety, as humanity. We need a name for this new belief. Perhaps transhumanism will serve: man remaining man, but transcending himself, by realizing new possibilities of and for his human nature."[8]

Transhumanism is something other than Nietzsche's position, which advocates self-overcoming for individuals capable and willing to do so. Transhumanists' objective is the self-transcendence of humanity as a whole, incarnating not just Nietzsche and Pindar's "become who you are" but rather "become more than you are."

Transhumanists have been careful to distance themselves from prior totalitarian projects that have attempted to modify the human race. They have embraced the flag of progressivism, and their proposals are increasingly tied to cultural liberalism, democracy, and egalitarianism. James Hughes, for example, describes biopolitics as an emerging political force. In *Citizen Cyborg*, he puts forth a "democratic transhumanism" that combines transhumanist biopolitics with social-democratic politics and economics and cultural liberalism. He believes we will achieve a better, posthuman future when we have rendered technology safe and available for all while respecting the rights of people to control their own bodies. The benefits will accrue to all, not simply to the élites, and the state has an essential role to play here.

On the opposite end are the bioconservatives, who are opposed to any use of technology to augment human capabilities or modify our biological nature. The bioconservative thesis would run something like this: "Even if it were technically possible and legally permissible for people to engage in biomedical enhancement, it would not be morally permissible for them to do so."[9] The ranks of the bioconservatives are not entirely clear, but a plausible list would include Leon Kass, president of Bush's Bioethics Council; Francis Fukuyama, who was a member of the same council and published the book *Our Posthuman Future*; and Michael Sandel, who has spread the bioconservative message in many works, among them *The Case against Perfection*.[10] Other bioethicists like George Annas, Lori Andrews, and Rosario Isasi have proposed legislation making heritable genetic modifications in human beings a crime against humanity.

For Allan Buchanan, the political divide between these two factions is not as evident as it seems. According to Buchanan, there is no such thing as a "pro-enhancement" position simply because no one is in favor of enhancement as such without knowing what it is, what is its context, and what consequences it might bring. Nor is "anti-enhancement" a plausible position: who would oppose improvement as such? Beyond this dichotomy, Buchanan sees a group that is simply "anti-anti-enhancement," who believe cases must be examined individually.[11] Included in this group would be Jonathan Glover, Savulescu, Agar, Brock, Bostrom, DeGrazia, Sanberg, Buchanan himself, and others.[12] They do not see a clear difference between traditional and biomedical methods of enhancement, or an ethical one between learning—which is, in the end, a physiological enhancement—and intervention.

Those opposed to enhancement consider that it would supplant the virtue of gratitude for the given, disparaging it in light of the possible. Its proponents counter rightly that there is no reason to consider sacred what is normal; that the normal is simply an abstraction from statistics that need not enjoy special moral status. To the point that the desire for enhancement is bound up with the desire to completely master the conditions of human existence, proponents argue that enhancement is not tantamount to the quest for perfection. Finally, proponents argue, against the charge that they are seeking immortality, that their object is an improved quality of life.

More striking is the accusation that enhancement may produce a stratified and individualistic society that would exclude the disabled and undermine distributive justice.[13] Both factions include those like Habermas and Annas who believe any hypothetical modification must not affect the germline and be passed down to future generations. In contrast, the anti-anti position accepts this possibility, but recognizes the dangers it represents and considers it inadvisable for the present.

Conversations on this topic now touch on such varied phenomena as athletic performance (where it is seen as a possible analogue to doping), romantic relations, cognitive enhancement, generic enhancement, GMO plants, and the genetic modification of animals. There are musicians who take beta-blockers to calm their nerves, students who take Ritalin to improve their test scores, and even caffeine and Modafinil are stimulants that have effects on cognitive performance. Already existing or soon-to-exist technologies that will radically transform human beings are virtual reality, preimplantation genetic diagnosis, genetic engineering, drugs to aid memory, concentration, insomnia, mood, and performance, cosmetic surgery, gender reassignment, prostheses, and anti-aging techniques. All of them give rise to ethical questions, but what concerns us here is moral enhancement.

Moral Bioenhancement without Harm to Others

Thomas Douglas and others have asked whether moral enhancement is permissible; in principle, as a powerful response
to the objections of conservatives, who allege that there are
forms of enhancement beneficial to some but that are inadmissible because of the harms they might cause to others. Their
objections pertain above all to what we might call "positional
goods": if one person gains intelligence, he will disadvantage
those deprived of such gains and will have more opportunities
to compete for a job, for example; if a normal person's stature is
increased, he will have more possibilities than those who remain within normal bounds. But, Douglas assures, there are
enhancements beneficial to both their recipients and others;
these strive not to create better people; instead, "a person morally enhances herself if she alters herself in a way that may reasonably be expected to result in her having morally better future
motives, taken in sum, than she would otherwise have had."[14]
This kind of enhancement, according to Douglas, can result in
harm for no one.

To clarify his position, he looks at two emotions that virtually all ethical postures support attenuating, representing as
they do a moral shortcoming: aversion to certain racial groups
and the impulse toward violent aggression. When these are
weakened, greater moral outcomes obtain.

The biomedical basis of such a possibility lies in those areas
of behavioral genetics and neuroscience that are increasingly
illuminating the substrates of aggression. Modifying these
would produce an acceptable form of moral enhancement.
There is evidence of the implication of a polymorphism in the
MOA-A gene in disturbances of the serotonin system that give
rise to hostile behavior. Racism has been examined to a lesser

degree, but a pair of functional MRI studies suggest that the amygdala plays an important role. The progress of the neuroscience points toward a future in which enhancements in these areas would be possible, and the moral improvements they represent would make them permissible for individuals.[15]

But if Douglas's position ably dismantles conservative objections, three questions remain open: whether what he proposes is scientifically possible, what kinds of procedures would be required to carry it out, and what the foreseeable consequences are.

An Ethical Imperative

Savulescu and Persson go beyond Douglas, saying that biomedical attempts to improve human morals are not only licit, but actually represent a moral imperative. Savulescu writes that an investigation of the prospects for moral bioenhancement is imperative precisely because, as pharmaceuticals, implants, and biological interventions improve cognitive capacities, advancing science and rewarding a small group with greater cognitive capacities than the rest, these more intelligent people can more easily harm others.[16] Cognitive enhancement demands moral enhancement to avoid such harm.

The weakness in this argument lies in the fact that for decades, it has been possible for a group of people to make use of scientific-technical means to destroy the earth. But this risk lies less with scientists than with those with sufficient political or economic power to access instruments of this kind: atomic energy or weapons of mass destruction. Cognitive enhancement might augment existing power, but it does not represent a novel risk.

This is perhaps why Savulescu and Persson refer elsewhere to the exponential growth of humanity's scientific and technical power and the possibility of destroying the earth.[17] Karl-Otto Apel and Hans Jonas already formulated this warning in the sixties and seventies of the past century. What, then, is new here?

According to Apel, the problem is that the consequences of science and technology are universal, while ethics is reducible to the microsphere and mesosphere, whereas what we need is a universal ethics of responsibility for the consequences of science and technology. The scientistic idea of the sciences as an axiologically neutral activity, however, has stood in the way of the founding of such a universal ethics.[18] Hans Jonas shared this preoccupation with the destructive power of science and technology and proposed his ethics of responsibility as a possible brake on it.[19]

But those we might call *moral ameliorists* do not call for a universal ethics; instead, they note that the pressures of evolution have not engendered a moral psychology that permits us to address the moral problems our new powers have created. Climate change and war demand a new morality, a preoccupation with what lies far away, with future generations, with all living beings. And yet our *moral motivation* continues to be concerned above all with the small group. The problem is the moral motivation of individuals and not the difficulty of constructing a universal ethics.

This has been true since the appearance of *homo sapiens*, whose history has been marked largely by small-group life. Evolution has permitted us to adapt to our physical, psychological, and social surroundings through moral dispositions that consist fundamentally in altruism and the capacity for cooperation.[20] The transition to agriculture required cooperation, technology, and a degree of trust sufficient to divide tasks and wait for months without recompense. As Darwin said, it was group selection that allowed us to overcome selfishness, because more cohesive groups were capable of following social norms, sharing emotions, creating and submitting to institutions, and following religions. All this is unique to humans. As Tomasello says, "You will never see two chimpanzees carry a log together." The capacity to cooperate is unique to the human race.[21]

And so, according to ameliorists, morality consists principally in the disposition to altruism, sympathy with others, the desire that their lives go well, and a bundle of sentiments that lie at the base of justice and impartiality, based fundamentally on the law of give-and-take.[22]

This version coincides with one of the *topoi* of evolutionary biology, evolutionary psychology, experimental mathematics, and neuroscientists. When the human brain was evolving, people lived in small groups that were able to survive thanks to internalized altruism and mutual aid; these moral traits were engraved on the mind and aided in the reproduction of the species. Despite Dawkins's arguments about the key role of selfishness in human conduct or Hamilton's notion of genetic altruism, human groups that have survived seem to have followed some kind of contractual model, with cooperation based on strong or indirect reciprocity or mutualism.[23]

Human beings are not endowed with maximizing rationality, even in economic terms; instead, the figure of *homo economicus* should be dispensed with in favor of *homo reciprocans*, man as giver and receiver, capable of reciprocating, cooperating, and moved by instincts and emotions as well as by calculations of maximum utility.[24]

This is evident in the famous ultimatum game, in which two players try to maximize their winnings keeping in mind that neither will accept what he takes to be an unjust humiliation.[25] Curiously, it is chimpanzees that seem to display a maximizing rationality. In experiments where the ultimatum game is adapted to them, proposers' offers are almost always selfish, and respondents almost always accept any offer that is greater than nothing. They are not, therefore, acting indiscriminately, but rather maximizing their benefit without resorting to secondary considerations.[26] People, on the other hand, tend to perceive as more reasonable a proposal that will be accepted by all, showing that mutual benefit is more acceptable than maximization at any cost.

Such forms of altruism demand that their practitioners be equipped with the following capacities: quantifying the costs of any altruistic gesture and the benefits that may be expected to ensue from it; recalling prior interactions and recognizing whether benefits should be expected on the basis of them; recognizing the dependency between giving and receiving; calculating how long benefits take to arrive; being ready to accept a day between the initial instance of giving and receiving; detecting those who violate norms of reciprocity; and punishing the dishonest to prevent future infractions.

As mankind has recognized the benefits of constant giving and receiving, it has crystallized into the norms of reciprocity that form the basis of our societies.

But for the past 40,000 years, the genetic and biological bases of the human race have hardly changed, while unprecedented cultural evolution has taken place thanks to the development of written and spoken language. And yet, even as our social and physical environments have changed, our morality remains oriented toward small groups and internal cooperation. We now live in a globalized world of societies with millions of citizens along with which must be counted future generations and nonhuman living beings. At the same time, the moral motivations of individuals remain unchanged. Is there not an imbalance between the moral demands of democratic institutions in the post-conventional level of the evolution of the moral conscience and the moral motivations of individuals, still governed by the most primitive codes of survival?

Hume states explicitly that "In general, it may be affirm'd, that there is no such passion in human minds, as the love of mankind, merely as such, independent of personal qualities, of services, or of relation to ourself."[27] For his part, Kant affirms that "Now the benevolence present in the love for all men is indeed the greatest in its *extent*, but the smallest in its *degree*; and when I say I take an interest in this man's well-being only out of my love for all men, the interest I take is as slight as an interest can be. I am only not indifferent with regard to him."[28]

Many authors are attempting at present to organize the emotional system of citizens to respond to the demands of a democratic society, from George E. Marcus's pioneering *The Sentimental Citizen: Emotion in Democratic Politics* to Sharon R. Krause's *Civil Passions: Moral Sentiment and Democratic Liberalism*, which attempts to frame impartiality as an emotion.[29]

There is a need, in these circumstances, to legislate in order to achieve effective change, but this is the job of politicians, and voters are uninterested in the problems of those far from them in space and time. What can be done to change the *moral motivations* of citizens so that they begin to care?

To respond, it is essential to clarify the meaning of the moral. Here, Savulescu is unambiguous: morality opens the possibility of building a society in which one's own purposes (prudential values) may coincide with what is best for all (moral values). "For it is a familiar idea that it is definitive of morality to harmonize the prudential ends of people, so that they be co-satisfiable."[30]

Improving this motivation demands moral education, but biomedicine has granted us novel means. We now recognize that our *moral dispositions* have a biological base in the emotions and are closely linked to our motivations. The emotions appear to be the oldest features of our brains and are frequently linked to survival instincts.[31]

Education has long attempted to steer the emotions, but after many centuries, success is still wanting. But our understanding of genetics and neurobiology is beginning to enable us to directly treat the biological basis of moral motivations through pharmaceuticals, implants, or external augmentation of the brain.

For the logic of give-and-take to function, there must be adequate mobilization of a group of emotions that include gratitude for favors received and the desire to return them, anger when another person does harm, the desire for reprisal (to dissuade future aggressions), remorse, guilt, shame, pride, admiration, contempt, and forgiveness. According to Savulescu and Persson, these emotions are useful when the majority of the population exhibits them. Strengthening them will permit a general *enhancement of moral motivations*. Savulescu's proposals in this regard center on *moral motivation and the need to improve it in order to act morally*. Education, discussion, and reason are important, but the emotions must be altered as well. Our *moral dispositions* are based on biology and are not a product of culture like languages or laws. Hence, for him and for other authors in the field, biomedical research into moral awareness must accompany education.

Is This Really a Promising Path?

Biomedical proposals for improving morality present virtualities and limits that must be considered. We will begin with the virtualities, which are above all diagnostic:

> (1) It is important to recognize that our moral dispositions have biological bases intended to influence the adaptive efficiency of individuals. They are, however,

susceptible to influence. If people react instinctively by failing to take an interest in or even rejecting outgroups because codes inscribed in the brain demand this, we must ask whether we wish to reinforce these codes or orient our actions differently.[32]

(2) These biological bases developed as a response to a vanished social and physical environment very different from the present one. This is a *topos* of neuroethics.

(3) The *evolution of our biological dispositions*, which prepares us to survive in certain situations, does not coincide with the *moral progress of our culture*. The human race seems not to have changed in genetic or biological terms in the last forty thousand years, while written and spoken language have led to great cultural innovation.

Perhaps this imbalance between rational conviction and debate and the motivations embodied in emotions formed thousands of years ago in the brain is the basis of that *moral dumbfounding* Jonathan Haidt speaks of when he avers that people form their moral judgments intuitively, automatically, and emotionally, and are for this reason unable to explain the reasons for their judgments when asked.[33] Perhaps this is the essence of the already-cited Latin dictum *Video meliora proboque, deteriora sequor.*

(4) The question of which dispositions we should reinforce inspires another fundamental question: What do we understand the *moral* to be, and must we look for the response in evolution alone? If morality is merely the variant forms of cooperation, then enhancement means nothing more than reinforcing this inborn tendency. Authors such as Haidt believe this, seeing

morality as a mechanism for maximizing societal utility rather than group utility.[34] Only groups capable of establishing commitment can rid themselves of free riders and thrive. From this perspective, biomedical interventions augment the moral sentiment. "Oxytocin bonds people to their groups, not to all of humanity. Mirror neurons help people empathize with others, but particularly those that share their moral matrix. It would be nice to believe that we humans were designed to love everyone unconditionally. Nice, but rather unlikely from an evolutionary perspective. Parochial love—love within groups—amplified by similarity, a sense of shared fate, and the suppression of free riders, may be the most we can accomplish," writes Haidt, concluding elsewhere, "Morality binds and blinds."[35]

In my view, the moral progress social consciousness has achieved in our time demands not only that promotion of ingroup cooperation that favors group selection, but also partakes of moral dispositions that take into account all human beings regardless of group affiliation. And it is with regard to the latter that we must cultivate the emotions through the cordial virtues.[36]

(5) Moral ameliorists are correct in noting the failures of education despite centuries of attempts and such grand historical figures as the Buddha, Confucius, Socrates, and Jesus along with millions of committed parents and teachers. This does not, however, signify that complementing education with biomedical measures is beyond discussion.

(6) There have been significant bioethical discoveries. Oxytocin promotes trust, selective serotonin reuptake inhibitors (SSRIs) aid cooperation and reduce aggression,

and Ritalin also inhibits aggression. Biological bases for antisocial personality disorder have been found, and criminality has been associated with an MAO mutation in the X chromosome, particularly when the subject in question comes from social deprivation.[37] Does that mean that bioethics is a fruitful avenue to improve moral motivations? Perhaps, but I see serious limits in it that must be overcome. First, research is still at an early stage, with its future directions and medium- and long-term consequences far from clear. We must proceed one step at a time, case by case, examining the means employed and their possible effectiveness, keeping in mind that, for example, a dose of oxytocin administered nasally is not the same as a genetic modification.

Even defenders of bioenhancement state that the imperative is to continue looking in this direction, not beginning to practice bioenhancement at present. This is broadly acceptable: it is undoubtedly a moral imperative to conduct research into anything that may empower human beings so long as it doesn't do them harm. But it must be weighed against the importance of concurrent research, with financing bodies and experts in the field deciding what are the most promising prospects for humanity.

Further, any intervention with an eye to enhancing the moral dispositions would need to obtain the carefully informed consent of its subjects. This principle is established in section one of the Nuremburg Code of 1947: "The voluntary consent of the human subject is absolutely essential." The same premise presides over the Belmont Report. The principle of consent reflects what Habermas has called "the ethical self-understanding of the species," which is rooted in its autonomy.

Defenders of moral bioenhancement would counter that the person desirous of an intervention to enhance his moral dispositions is already driven by moral motivations. His desire would be to align his affects with moral interests, but this runs into difficulties when he attempts to align his conduct with reasoned convictions. In effect, there is little difference between inhaling oxytocin to promote trust and ingesting lithium to treat bipolar disorder, despite the fact that we call one an enhancement and the other therapy.

However, what moral ameliorists are most concerned with is strengthening the moral motivations of those who are *not* interested in acting morally. This ambition has three possible solutions: the state may offer incentives to those willing to act as guinea pigs; it may develop a moral improvement plan for the entire population; or each country's educational ministries could develop a protocol for improving the moral motivations of children. The first would place us in a new version of *A Clockwork Orange*, and reveals the risk of depersonalization run by whoever submits to behavioral or motivational modifications for external incentives. The second brings us before the danger of authoritarian eugenics, however much moral ameliorists insist that legislation must respect the demands of democracy. The fact that the need of moral enhancement is being trumpeted with reference to the risks the planet and future generations are facing and the supposition that these demand people possessed of moral motivations at the post-conventional level of the development of moral conscience leads one to fear that its proponents are seeking some form of state planning, whether or not it is their stated aim.

We might recall here the "liberal euthanasia" that has arisen in this century and attempts to distinguish itself from the authoritarian eugenics of the past by imposing the following

conditions: a neutral state rather than one that frames and im-
poses eugenic laws; an extension rather than a curtailment of
procreative rights; expert genetic counselors who support parents and are not agents of the state; a goal of individual enhancement rather than racial purity; an emphasis on economic
efficiency rather than political ideology; and the imperative
that, as with education, the right to decide lies with the parents
rather than the state.[38]

The problem is that complementing the education process—
with school planning organized by the state—remains uncom-
fortably close to nonconsensual modification of another person's behavior. If even in the case of violent persons, it is
considered ethically problematic to intervene in their physiol-
ogy to reduce their aggressive disposition, the application of
bioenhancement to children within an educational framework
is an intolerable resort to statism reminiscent of such dystopias
as Aldous Huxley's *Brave New World*.

Nor is a modification of the motives for cooperation tantamount to a modification of morality as such. Moral motives in
interactions with others near and far demands a cultivation of
the capacity to appreciate what is inherently valuable, not simply that which may be beneficial for life in common. This is
what Kant calls the sentiment of respect before that which is an
end in itself. It is essential to make this sentiment an unavoidable
part of life, and I do not see how biomedical means can do this.

Bioenhancement for now sounds like science fiction, but it
may eventually become a reality, and citizens should be aware
of it and take part in debates surrounding it. It is essential here
to ask: Is there no other road apart from biological interventions to convince humanity of the importance of virtue? Might
it even be that there is no moral chip, no drug or implant to

substitute for the patient, voluntary education of the character of individuals, institutions, and peoples?

There seems to be no avoiding the task of shaping individual and social conscience through formal and informal education and the construction of suitable institutions, as we will see in the following chapter. And we cannot forget that shared experiences of suffering and joy, of shared compassion, are the best school of all.

To quote Kant, a man often unjustly accused of giving short shrift to the sentiments:

> But while it is not in itself a duty to share the sufferings (as well as the joy) of others, it is a duty to sympathize actively in their fate; and to this end it is therefore an indirect duty to cultivate the natural (aesthetic [*ästhetische*]) feelings in us, and to make use of them as so many means to sympathy based on moral principles and the feeling appropriate to them. It is therefore a duty not to avoid the places where the poor who lack the most basic necessities are to be found but rather to seek them out, and not to shun sick-rooms or debtors' prisons and so forth in order to avoid sharing painful feelings one may not be able to resist. For this is still one of the impulses that nature has implanted in us to do what the representation of duty alone would not accomplish.[39]

Chapter 7

Erradicating Poverty, Reducing Inequality

Of the corruption of our moral sentiments, which is occasioned
by this disposition to admire the rich and the great, and to
despise or neglect persons of poor and mean condition.[1]

The Poor Person in the Exchange Society

Throughout this book, we have described as poor those who
seem incapable of offering anything in societies that are based
on exchange; who cannot participate in the reciprocal act of
giving and receiving, whether directly from the beneficiary of
these acts or indirectly from another. This is the key to our contractualist societies, which are clearly superior to those governed by rampant selfishness, but which also exclude the poor,
submitting them to the principle of exchange as well as the
aforementioned Matthew principle.

In an exchange-based world, the poor are rejected because
they bring only problems to those trying to prosper, breed contempt when contemplated from a position of superiority, stoke
fear when they produce insecurity, and are, at the least, tolerated

with an impatience among those hoping one way or another to get rid of them. Hatento is right to accompany their case studies with illustrations of apparently empty streets, signaling with question marks the places where there are homeless beggars. These people aren't invisible as such—they have been made that way.

As rejection is coded by evolution in the brain, overcoming it demands the cultivation of productive compassion. Compassion is more than just give-and-take: it is above all the recognition of another as an equal, connected to us by a tie that antecedes any pact or agreement. But if our brain is aporophobic, and we are born with a tendency to reject those who seem to offer us no benefit, all people must work for this change throughout the course of their lives.

The transition toward egalitarian ideals requires education within the family, through the media, and in all aspects of public life, as well as the development not only of just institutions, but of institutions that build just characters. Irrespective of the nature of the tasks such bodies carry out, their mere existence has a pedagogical force and influences people's brains and their social and personal character.

Such political, educational, and cultural organizations should work to foment a neurodemocracy opposed to the hatred of the poor and the ill positioned. And yet this is not enough, because the economy, too, has extraordinary weight in terms of shaping our ways of thinking and acting. It is no surprise that Adam Smith, professor of moral philosophy for thirteen years at the University of Glasgow and author of *An Inquiry into the Nature and Causes of the Wealth of Nations*, was likewise author of *The Theory of Moral Sentiments*, which contains a reflection on the corruption of the moral sentiments by the tendency to admire the rich and despise the poor, the title of which precedes the present chapter.

What he describes is similar to present-day aporophobia, and the following complaint of Smith's is familiar to us as well: "That wealth and greatness are often regarded with the respect and admiration which are due only to wisdom and virtue; and that the contempt, of which vice and folly are the only proper objects, is often most unjustly bestowed upon poverty and weakness, has been the complaint of moralists in all ages."[2] Many today feel this tendency should be channeled into respect for the equal dignity of persons, and doing this demands a reconception of economic institutions. Economics is the science of attempting to overcome scarcity, but even more, *the science of eliminating poverty*. And so we must ask: Is eliminating poverty a duty to justice or a charitable obligation?

Is Justice Obligated to Eradicate Economic Poverty?

Throughout human history, there have been people, groups, associations, and institutions that have worked to eliminate poverty. But beyond these voluntary approaches, it may be understood as a duty to justice required of political powers such as individual states, the European Union, the United Nations, and systems of global governance. This must be closely coordinated with the businesses and economic and financial institutions that are responsible for creating material and immaterial wealth. To clarify whether this is a question of justice or charity, four sets of questions must be resolved:

(1) Who are the poor, from an economic point of view?

(2) Is poverty inevitable, or must humanity grow accustomed to it and merely attempt to reduce incidence of it, as we do with disease?

(3) Are societies obligated to offer their citizens equality of outcomes? Is this a question of rights or of utilitarian calculations? Are anti-poverty measures a question of promotion or protection? Does justice oblige us to empower those who are poor against their will to emerge from poverty because it is intrinsically bad, or are we seeking to defend the poor from the worst blows of fortune while protecting society against the negative externalities of poverty?

(4) Is it sufficient to eliminate poverty, or must we also attempt to reduce inequality?

Poverty Is a Lack of Freedom

Determining who counts as poor is a thorny task but one necessary to determine whether we have progressed in the struggle against poverty. Measures such as the poverty line attempt to assign quantitative values to who is and is not poor: a politician or researcher selects a set of essential goods and their price and calls poor whoever lacks the money to attain them. Others look at the average income and expenditure of a region, divide this by two, and declare poor those who fail to reach this amount. These measurements change with time and must be regularly updated.[3] There are also distinct degrees of poverty. The World Bank considers extreme poverty an income of less than $1.25 per day in 2005 dollars, and moderate poverty one of less than two dollars per day.

The quantitative approach has its virtues, but there is much that it leaves out, and numerous critiques have been leveled against monetary measurements. The same goods may not serve the same basic needs in different places: the need for shelter is more pressing in the poles than in the tropics, and money has different value in a developed society than in one where informal economies predominate. Context is essential for determining the poverty line; for this reason, some speak of "clinical economics" or "hermeneutical economics."[4] Further, monetary metrics' fixation on goods required to satisfy basic necessities can become a kind of fetish that fails to grasp whether these goods are actually relieving poverty. Finally, these metrics only look at the aggregate, not at comparisons of wealth between people.[5]

More adequate, then, are complex indices that consider not only income and consumption, but also variables like literacy, life expectancy, infant mortality, shelter, nutrition, and the environment. In line with these, Jeffrey Sachs and others have distinguished three levels of poverty: (1) Extreme or absolute poverty, in which families are incapable of satisfying their basic needs and cannot escape poverty without aid from others. This only exists in developing countries. (2) Moderate poverty, when basic necessities are covered, but precariously. (3) Relative poverty, when the family income level is lower than a certain proportion of the national average.[6]

Amartya Sen has given another, very incisive definition of poverty: it is, in the end, a lack of freedom.[7]

In cases of extreme poverty, first things must come first.[8] This means, in line with the hierarchy of human needs, that the first step in eliminating it is addressing these needs and freeing oneself from them.[9] Moving from here to a broader definition of poverty, we must consider those who lack freedom, who lack the capacity to bring into being their chosen life plans or control their lives in any substantive way. Such people are not agents, but subjects of a social or environmental lottery in which one cannot pursue happiness according to one's dispositions.

Poverty introduces negative discrimination between people in such basic matters as organizing their lives and pursuing happiness, because only certain human beings have the means to do so. And so again, we ask the question: Does justice oblige us to furnish such opportunities, so that people may be autonomous and not heteronomous, capable of striving after happiness in their own ways? This question only makes sense, however, if poverty is avoidable in the twenty-first century.

Poverty Is Avoidable

The poor ... are like the shadows in a painting: they provide the necessary contrast.

—PHILIPPE HECQUET, 1740

Our dream is a world free of poverty.

—MOTTO OF THE WORLD BANK SINCE 1990[10]

Though some constitutions ensure the right to happiness, such a right does not exist as such, and declarations concerning it are merely hot air. Greek ethics worked to articulate which virtues a person should cultivate to make intelligent decisions in the search for the good life and to foster good character, keeping in mind that we are all in fate's hands. Happiness must navigate the voluntary formation of character and involuntary fortune, which is *what happens to a person* as opposed to *what a person does*. We are hybrids of autonomy and vulnerability.[11]

The Greeks understood clearly that the good life did not depend on riches, and possession of riches was no virtue. Aristotle realized that the possession of certain material goods was necessary to dedicate oneself to a life of contemplation, but wealth was not happiness. The moral schools that succeeded him—the

Epicureans, the Stoics, and the Cynics—agreed that autarky, the ability to rule oneself, was the authentic good, and that it was irrational to covet riches. For the Stoics, the wise man does not regret his poverty, because being rich or poor is out of his hands. Wisdom consists of searching for happiness through that which does depend upon us.

Seneca and others even argued that poverty could be a good, because riches were an obstacle to the refinement of the spirit. In his letter to Lucilius on philosophy and riches, he would advise against seeking wealth for one who wished to devote his life to philosophy. Indeed, he remarks, poverty is desirable because the poor person is content to satisfy his most pressing needs and then to consign himself to the work of the spirit. Quoting Epicurus to the effect that "the acquisition of riches has been for many men, not an end, but a change, of troubles," he states that for the philosopher's vocation, one must "either be a poor man, or resemble a poor man" through frugality, which is "voluntary poverty." Wisdom, he declares, is the prize of the man for whom wealth is superfluous.[12] In *On Worldly Deception*, he advises Lucilius once more to eschew the fear of poverty, because the poor do not have the worries of the rich, and for them, "the mind grows from within, giving to itself nourishment and exercise. . . . All that goes to make you a good man lies within yourself."[13]

These reflections are suggestive for social movements that promote new ways of life and consumption as a challenge to rampant capitalism in which the consumer is the motor of production.[14] They also fit the stoic model of life, however much Seneca himself seems not to have opted for the life of poverty he recommended to Lucilius. Still, it is essential to note that he is speaking of voluntary and not involuntary poverty, and that the ancient world in both the East and the West understood involuntary poverty as an obstacle to agency in one's own life and an evil for those who suffered it. For them, it was an *unavoidable evil*. The conviction was widespread that there would always be poor people, and that poverty was not caused by social injustices that it was imperative to ameliorate. This is far from the perspective that involuntary poverty has its roots in society and that the poor person has a right to demand society's help in attaining the good life, which will not appear until the eighteenth century, with the appearance of what Ravallion calls "the first Poverty Enlightenment," which argued that poverty was avoidable.

Until a few centuries ago, poverty was the general human condition. The generation of indefinite wealth is a recent outgrowth of the combination of new industrial technologies, fossil fuels, market forces, social mobility, urbanization, changing family structures, and the division of labor. Accompanying all this were political developments that aided mobility and progress, like the appearance of parliamentarianism in Great Britain and the social contract theories which, following Hobbes, understood society as a voluntary association of citizens, secularizing the notion of natural rights and making their protection the responsibility of the state, which was being born as a political entity at that time.[15]

All this has led, in the past hundred eighty years, to a multiplication by forty-nine of the economic activity of the planet, generating sufficient resources to eradicate hunger. The Malthusian position, that population growth must necessarily strain resources, has waned in the face of Condorcet's belief that indefinite progress creates indefinite wealth.

Involuntary poverty is avoidable. As the former president of the Society for the Study of Economic Inequality, Martin Ravallion, shows in *The Economics of Poverty*, thinking about poverty has changed dramatically since writers first took up the subject, as we can see contrasting the two quotations that begin this section.[16] Ravallion points out two transitional stages in our thinking about poverty—the First and Second Poverty Enlightenments—each of which lasts approximately twenty years.[17] The first takes place at the end of the eighteenth century and frames respect for the poor as a social question rather than a personal one: here, the conclusion appears that the economy must generate prosperity for the poor as well as others. Adam Smith is one of the main proponents of this view. This lays the groundwork for the idea that all people have dignity, that this is something more than economic value, that they are ends in themselves and must not be used as instruments. The Kantian Formula of the End in Itself is the highest formulation of this demand that the poor be empowered and the state act on their behalf.[18]

In the Second Poverty Enlightenment, poverty comes to be seen not as inevitable, but as an ill to be eliminated, and doing so is now perceived as a responsibility of the state. This occurs in the 1960s and 1970s, when the belief spreads that poverty is a restriction on personal freedom and self-satisfaction— perhaps the most significant restriction of all. A consensus appears that poverty is unacceptable, even as debates continue about what should be done to relieve it.

It was heartening for this reason that in 2000, when the United Nations announced its Millennium Development Goals, which were intended to be reached by 2015, the first of these was eradicating extreme poverty and hunger. The other seven were urgent as well, but extreme poverty and hunger make the achievement of any other goal impossible. In 2015, the UN proposed its Sustainable Development Goals, to be accomplished by 2030, and at the top of the list was simply "No poverty."

Not reducing it, but ending it, with the help of economic, business, and political organizations.

Not Just Protecting Society but, above All, Empowering People

Anti-poverty policies may be considered means of protecting people or societies or as means of promoting persons.[19] As means of protecting individuals, they allow the satisfaction of the most basic necessities, and are justified when they avoid the loss of life. But once the basic necessities are covered, anti-poverty measures may make poverty chronic, running the risk of falling into the "poverty trap" whereby people make enough to survive but not to escape poverty. Many populist policies lead people into this trap, stymying their progress and forcing them to depend entirely on their supposed benefactors, for whom they vote unconditionally because their lives depend on it. This is the opposite of what autonomous citizenship should be, and so good anti-poverty policies will try to help people escape poverty.

The divergent notion that anti-poverty policies protect society has been frequently encountered throughout history. They were seen in the ancient world in several periods when poverty was understood to produce social conflicts, insecurity, and delinquency. In 500 BCE, Confucius described poverty as one of the six calamities that the government was obliged to avoid in order to preserve social order. Chanakya counseled kings in his *Arthashastra*, written three hundred years before the birth of Christ, to develop policies of social preservation that would maintain the stability of their regimes; but these policies explicitly favored hierarchy and inequality.[20]

Aristotle believed a natural hierarchy existed among men, with the slave subordinate to the master and the woman to the man, and he felt it best for all that those endowed with reason govern. As for the poor, he deems their place in political life among the masses, whom he associates with democracy, and avers that they ought not govern because they are a decadent people who struggle to submit to reason. For him, a government of the middle class is preferable.[21] (He does recognize a certain kinship between master and slave; it does not extend to the animal.)[22]

In the early sixteenth century, policies seeking to protect the poor and, by extension, society gathered weight. In Britain and Europe, the numbers of the poor, beggars, highwaymen, prostitutes, and witches grew immensely, and pauperism was deemed a threat to the social order. In this context, the first treatise on poverty was published in 1526. Bruges asked a celebrated humanist, the Valencian Juan Luis Vives, to write it, and hence the text of *De subventione pauperum* (*On the Relief of the Poor*) was born from the pen of one of the most esteemed students of the university of Valencia.

The book's stated purpose is to verify the numbers of the poor and in this way propose measures for their alleviation in a rational way. The fundamental intention is to protect society from thieves, infectious diseases, maledictions, and rogues, matters which "must not be despised by those who govern the people, who would do well to remedy these ills to prevent their spilling over to the many. He is no wise governor nor lover of the common good who allows so great a part of the citizenry as the poor to remain not only useless, but indeed harmful to themselves and others."[23]

His treatise is not content to analyze the situation of the poor and propose measures to avoid their plight spreading through the rest of society. It also expressly recognizes that "it is an embarrassment to us Christians, who care for charity above all else, indeed, whose sole duty is charity, in my view, to allow the poor and indigent to remain among us wherever we step. No matter where you look, you will see a thousand poor and a thousand needy, a thousand hands forced to reach out from poverty."[24]

Luis Vives took a great step forward in the fight against poverty by asserting that charity and individual almsgiving were not enough, and that public power—municipal power, in the case of his text—must step in and study the situation. As Muñoz Machado writes, Vives's proposals "stood apart from traditional charitable practices and were oriented toward the bureaucratization of social assistance at the municipal level."[25] This was the origin of the First Poverty Enlightenment and the roots of the welfare state that would appear centuries later.

The English Old Poor Laws of the sixteenth century served protection more than promotion, prohibiting the distribution of wealth or the overcoming of the poverty trap, but they did displace private almsgiving in favor of social protection. Not until the Second Poverty Enlightenment in the 1960s and 1970s would anti-poverty measures (higher salaries, educational systems, rational financial markets) move away from *protecting* the political regime and social stability to *promoting* poor people so that they might emerge from poverty.[26]

Charity or Justice?

The idea that poverty is avoidable because the means exist to eradicate it does not signify that attempting to do so is a moral duty. Realizing that something can be done doesn't imply that it ought to be done; instead, the path from capability to duty requires an intervention of the personal or social conscience that dictates that the poor person has a right not to be poor and that society ought to empower him to emerge from poverty.

Fortunately, the understanding that eliminating poverty is a duty for humanity is worldwide, and international activism in favor of doing just that is on the rise.[27] Still, this is a recent phenomenon.

It was the monotheistic religions—Judaism, Christianity, Islam—that presented poverty as a problem and made sharing one's goods to help eliminate it a principle of faith.[28] In the Old Testament, Yahweh inveighs against those who neglect the poor, orphans, and widows, the *aporoi*. His message is implacable and insistent: "For I desired mercy, and not sacrifice." Care for the *aporoi* is, along with the worship of Yahweh, *the orthopraxis* or authentic practice of the religion, and the prophets emphasize it, even at the risk of their lives. Unsurprisingly, Habermas appeals to the Jewish roots of German idealism as one of the central currents of critical theory when he says, "The Jews' German idealism produces the leaven of a critical utopia." Michael Walzer likewise depicts the way of the prophets as a possibility of hermeneutics.[29]

The New Testament opens the doors to the Kingdom to those who fed the hungry, gave drink to the thirsty, and sheltered the wayfarer. And in a world where there are poor and rich, it blesses the first. The Sermon on the Mount is open to many interpretations, but there is no denying that the attention it pays to the meek and downtrodden is the essence of Christianity.[30]

Is any of this charity, alms? Clearly not—it must instead be called justice. It is simply demanded of the individual and the group rather than the political community. Hence the many medieval Christian rebellions that demanded attention to the poor and the purification of the Church—for example that of Thomas Münzer, mentioned by Marx, Engels, and Block— were pioneering.

In the Middle Ages and the Renaissance, the discourse of personal rights and of the polity's obligations to its citizenry had yet to become a fact of life. With Luis Vives's text on the poor, public powers are finally entreated to intervene to avoid the spread of poverty because it is unchristian to ignore the needs of the poor; but there is as yet no belief that the poor have a right to emerge from poverty and that the community is obliged to respect that right.

This is rather a peculiar trait of the modern world, which has frequently and rightly been characterized as the age of the individual: unlike the foregoing eras, the modern world centers the individual and his rights.[31] The desire to see these rights protected is what seals, in theory, the contract by which the state is born, with citizens agreeing to perform their duties so long as the state protects their rights. This primitive version of the rule of law is born in the seventeenth and eighteenth centuries.

The Right to a Free Life

The recognition of the right to emerge from poverty, and of society's obligation to help in this process, has a history rooted in the eighteenth-century affirmation that every human being has dignity; but it is not until the twentieth century that the legal consequences of this affirmation are brought to light. In the nineteenth century, the "social question" referred above all to factory exploitation, not to the need to do away with poverty and hunger. Only in the 1948 Universal Declaration of Human Rights does the individual's right to life come to imply a corollary—namely, the obligation of national and international bodies to ensure it.[32]

This document follows the deontological tradition founded by Kant in the eighteenth century and refuses to submit individual rights to utilitarian calculations. Unlike Bentham, who contends that there is no right that cannot be abrogated if doing so betters the lot of the community, deontology defends the priority of individual rights in the face of collective utility, giving priority to human dignity. Rawls will add to the Kantian tradition by drawing a distinction between deontology and teleology in his theory of justice, which rests on two fundamental principles: the idea of the just and the idea of the good, either of which may be taken as a point of departure. If we choose what is good for the citizens (pleasure, utility), the just will consist of maximizing this good, as utilitarianism has traditionally attempted to do with the theories of Bentham and welfare economics. Bentham considers talk of human rights "nonsense on stilts" and affirms there is no right that cannot be abolished so long as doing so redounds to the general good. His was certainly a revolutionary and transformative position, but it is profoundly deficient as a theory of justice for its negligence of the rights of individuals.

Deontology, on the other hand, takes the rights of citizens as the departure point for a theory of justice and considers them to provide the framework within which each person designs the project of a good and happy life. For this reason, it affirms that the just takes priority over the good.

Drawing on an idea of the social contract in which citizens decide which principles for them represent justice, Rawls will propose a number of ideas: that society is obliged to guarantee its citizens certain material minimums, certain rights and liberties that are beyond debate, the social bases of self-esteem, equality of opportunities, and the social organization that best protects the rights of the least advantaged. These primary goods are those that any person would wish to possess in order to carry out any life project. And a society could be called just if the distribution of burdens and benefits within it is such that no other one could be described as more beneficial for the least advantaged.

Sen finds himself in a similar deontological line when he asks in a well-known article, "Equality of What?" Since the 1970s, thinkers have sought to answer this question, not always within the domain of economics alone, and they agree that the equal consideration and respect human beings deserve demands the enactment of a *social equality*, whether in terms of basic goods (Rawls), the satisfaction of basic needs (Streeten, Galtung, Gasper), in certain resources (Dworkin), in the protection of human rights (Pogge), or in the empowerment of basic capacities (Sen, Nussbaum, Crocker, Comim, Pereira).

In all these cases, it goes without saying that eradicating poverty and reducing inequality are essential goals in the economies of the twenty-first centuries.

Reducing Inequality: Proposals for the Twenty-First Century

In this period, known as the Information Age, the Communication Age, the Access Age, the Digital Age, or the Age of Sustainable Development, the economy faces the following challenges:

Asymmetrical globalization as a reaction of neoliberalism to the welfare state, with its benefits accruing to different classes in different degrees, generating inequality, hunger, and exclusion; the absence of a concurrent global politics and ethics that would distribute the benefits of globalization to the people; the financialization of the economy to the detriment of the real economy, which raises uncertainty and distorts the tasks of the business and financial sectors;[33] the multipolar configuration of the new geopolitical order, in which emerging countries are gaining political and economic power in fits and starts;[34] the crisis of political refugees and poor immigrants, which is as old as humanity itself, but has taken on immense proportions in our day and supposes a radical test for our sense of justice; the challenge of new technologies, the progress of digitalization, and the need for sustainable development that serves the environment as well as people;[35] the persistence of poverty and unjust inequalities in a world with sufficient resources to eliminate them.

In the face of these, proposals like the following are essential:

First, *reducing inequalities* in order to eradicate poverty and create growth. Poverty is avoidable and the duty to eliminate it lies not with the danger that a world of poor people would pose for the well-off; it is not a protective measure against the negative externalities of poverty. It may be that poverty has a serious economic and political impact because people who don't work don't produce, and poor citizens don't participate in politics; there is, then, a virtuous circle in the reduction of poverty, just distribution, and economic growth.[36] But the question isn't simply one of strategy and prudence, but also of justice: people have the right to a life without poverty, and societies have the duty to give them the means to achieve it. This follows from the recognition that human beings possess dignity. Ensuring this right has positive repercussions for social peace, but helping people out of the poverty trap is the necessary response to their right to live in liberty.

But to empower the poor, it is necessary to overcome such external factors as incomplete markets, inadequate governments, and unequal access to productive or financial inputs. This is why some have said that perhaps the greatest challenge consists of reducing inequalities, which are undesirable on their own and because of the poverty they generate. As Alfonso Novales writes, if inequality rises, wealth eludes the poor and heightened inequality makes even growth difficult. According to the seven hundred experts who contributed to the report *Global Risks 2014* for the Davos World Economic Forum, income inequality may be the most important factor in the world economy in the coming decade, more so than climate change, unemployment, fiscal crises, and geopolitical risks.[37]

Research into the causes of inequality is one of the central—and controversial—themes of the work of Thomas Piketty, who describes how high rates of return on capital can increase inequality.[38] This is an injustice on its own, but it also has grave consequences: citizens lose faith in a system that treats them unjustly; high inequality is a brake on growth; and political and economic institutions channel wealth toward the favored and powerful.[39]

The diversion of rents toward the powerful is what has been called clientelism, and it is an obstacle to achieving equality of opportunity. Not only is it inherently asymmetrical, giving opportunities to some and denying them to others, but it generates poverty by using public resources inefficiently. It follows that this kind of corruption is not only immoral as such, but likewise limits growth. We see, therefore, that the timeworn dichotomy between pro-growth and pro-equality policies is a false one.[40]

Reducing inequalities is one of the central objectives of the current century. To address inequalities between countries, this requires development aid following a codevelopment model that avoids flooding developing countries with unwanted customs and unnecessary goods that stymie their own capacities while salving the conscience of donor countries. Development measures driven by those affected by them is the only way to act efficiently and justly.[41] But we mustn't forget that the best assistance is not freighting goods from worse-off countries with tariffs to protect the home market.

Within countries, clientelism and corruption must be eliminated through efficient and effective transparency measures; the real economy must be favored over finance; tax systems must be truly progressive; welfare state policies must be reinforced along with such policies as universal basic income, which permit a measure of freedom to all.[42] Equality of opportunity requires equal access to education and health care, to credit to develop business projects or finance the accumulation of human capital, and to equal treatment before the law.[43]

Economic institutions that eliminate poverty and reduce inequality are the best way to eradicate aporophobia.

Second, economic power must be brought in line with universal ideals in a globalized world. The economy, linked to the *oikos*, the home, in the fourth century BCE (Aristotle), concerned itself in the modern era with the wealth and poverty of nations (Adam Smith), and is now entering a global context that it has helped to develop. Globalization has been made possible through the progress of information technologies and the expansion of the economy, particularly through the enhanced mobility of financial markets.

The intelligent and just thing to do at this moment is make use of our resources to bring to life those values our civilization aspires to, the values of civic ethics that form part of the core of any social undertaking and must be translated into good practices. These values, being shared among morally pluralistic societies, are becoming transnational. It is therefore essential to promote such measures as the United Nations Global Compact, proposed in 1999 at the Davos Economic Forum by Secretary General Kofi Annan:

> Let's combine the power of markets with the authority of universal values, and the creative power of the entrepreneur with the needs of the left-behind and future generations.

The Millennium Sustainable Development Goals and the Sustainable Development Goals likewise encourage businesses to become local and global citizens.[44]

Also important is the adoption of John Ruggie's Guiding Principles of protect, respect, and remedy, which appeal to governments and firms to defend human rights. Governments must protect human rights, but businesses are obliged to respect them and remedy harms done to them. They should also do what is in their power to help change deficient legislation, using their influence to become agents of justice.[45]

Third, Corporate Social Responsibility (CSR) should be adopted as a question not merely of appearance, but of justice and prudence. We do not agree with those who consider this to be an instance of "enlightened self-interest." Rather, it is an exercise of the virtue of prudence, which, according to Aristotle, is practical knowledge about how to live well. We should moreover broaden the term "stakeholders" to include those "affected by the activities of a firm and who possess legitimate expectations with regard to them."[46]

CSR, even if it has received justified criticism, is a beneficial tool for management, a prudential measure that justice demands.[47] This is true for SMEs as well as for large firms and megacorporations. It uses the tangible and intangible wealth of companies to build a better society. Corporate benefits must serve ends beyond corporate survival; they must remain competitive in uncertain environments, but following legitimate and intelligent principles—and nothing is more beneficial for their long-term survival than attempting to benefit everyone affected by their activities.

Thus, as Jesús Conill writes, the best business models are based not around ruthless profit maximization for stockholders or institutional service on a contractual basis, but take as broad a view as possible of their beneficiaries and obligations, seeking to increase alliances and reduce adversaries, in line with the criteria of prudence and justice.[48]

Fourth, business models must be invested with a pluralistic ethic, which is advantageous not only to individuals and political bodies, but also to firms. Pluralistic economies set conditions for mercantile activities, but also regulate economic entities that are capable of generating added value without pursuing profit and therefore produce wealth.[49] We must encourage not only conventional profit-seeking enterprises, but also activities at the margins of conventional business whose priority is satisfying social needs and avoiding exclusion. José Ángel Moreno calls these the "seeds of an alternative economy," new models of commerce, consumption, and investment. Their purpose is to build a new world through economic activity.[50] In 2009, Pérez de Mendiguren dubbed this "social and solidary economics."

Such companies take as their goals the empowerment of individuals, the prioritization of cooperation over competition, democratic decision-making, care for the environment, job creation, and ethical action.[51] Their ranks include traditional social enterprises, social or solidary firms, the Economy for the Common Good, the collaborative economy, which shares not only property but means of production and local currencies, and alternative finance with a social investment focus.

These measures have been the source of dispute, and yet they are producing many jobs and a great deal of material wealth. They provide a meeting point between the social and economic sectors, and may offer a propitious avenue for empowering the poor.[52]

Fifth, businesses and the economy as a whole must pursue rational economic motives. It is often stated that self-interest is the motor of the economy, following Adam Smith's famous assertion that "it is not from the benevolence of the butcher, the brewer, or the baker that we expect our dinner, but from their regard to their own self-interest. We address ourselves not to their humanity but to their self-love, and never talk to them of our own necessities, but of their advantages."[53] But acting from self-interest alone is suicide. Reciprocity and cooperation are equally essential, as are the ability to honor contracts and create stable institutions. We must foment the commitment to eliminating poverty, empowering the poor through recognition of their dignity, and care for the environment, which is increasingly vulnerable in our day.[54]

Promoting pluralism of motivations in economic activity in the twenty-first century—not just self-interest, but sympathy and commitment—will strengthen the economy in line with the principles of the market and the cognitive bases of rationality and the economic impulses outlined in the works of the neuroeconomists.[55] These have discredited the idea of *homo economicus* as an individualist seeking to maximize benefits in thrall to evolutionary impulses based around the struggle for survival and eliminating enemies. People are rather a hybrid of *homo economicus* and *homo reciprocans*, with a knowledge of how to cooperate and to distinguish between those who honor and violate contracts and a willingness to reward the one and punish the other.

Contractual rationality may be indispensable to public life, but being restricted to already existing agreements, it does not seek to transcend itself in seeking out those excluded from the cycle of reciprocity. It excludes the *aporoi*, and in this way fails to reach a large part of those affected by economic activity.

An ethic of cordiality, on the other hand, recognizes the value of contracts for public, economic, and social life, but sees their roots as lying in a more basic form of human tie: the alliance. An alliance implies mutual recognition among people endowed with dignity as vulnerable creatures that require justice, care, and compassion.[56]

Chapter 8

Cosmopolitan Hospitality

Asylum and the Refugee Crisis

In his *Pedagogy*, Kant affirms that "Man can only become man by education. He is what education makes of him."[1] For him, there are two particularly difficult problems for humanity: the government of societies and education. The second he considers more complex than the first, because we must decide whether to educate for the present moment or for a better future that we must anticipate creatively. He opted to educate for a better future, a cosmopolitan society where no one feels excluded. This represents a peace very necessary today when wars are destroying lives and entire cities in places like Syria, Afghanistan, Iraq, Libya, Israel, and Palestine, apart from the terrorist attacks in all corners of the globe.

Such conflicts add to the problem of refugees to that of poor immigrants. The aporophobia expressed toward these groups is often embodied in hate speech perpetrated by political parties and populist groups that recall the attitudes of hunter-gatherers hostile to outsiders and willing to defend their group hair, tooth, and nail. As our brain structure hasn't evolved through the centuries, these groups persist in a biological selfishness that ignores the moral progress of humanity's conscience; they insist on closing borders to impede the flow of those fleeing unbearable pain.

The exodus of economic migrants and political refugees is one of the greatest challenges in the globalized world at the mesolevel of national institutions and the macrolevel of international institutions. It therefore demands a collaborative solution.

Economic migration has increased exponentially because of the poverty plaguing the African continent, which obliges its citizens to flee their countries, crossing the Mediterranean for the coasts of Italy, Greece, and Spain. This is a world of mafias, of rafts loaded with men, women, and children, of death at sea, of shipwrecks, of fences, of detention centers, the first of which opened in 2012 in Greece with intended processing periods of just a few days. Riots and protests in these centers have risen in recent times, citing the inhuman conditions inside them and the long periods of detention.

It is a problem of many dimensions. What the UN's 1951 Refugee Convention describes as the "well-founded fear of being persecuted for reasons of race, religion, nationality, membership of a particular social group, or political opinion" includes the need to resort to mafias, border security in the target countries, and judicial the loss of life, the suffering of abandoning a war-torn home country, and hurdles related to asylum status. These are the consequence of a lack of clarity or common approaches in the EU with regard to this humanitarian crisis, which has meant that member countries focus on their perceptions of their own problems and lack a capacity for common response, with their positions changing by the day.

Jihadist attacks have only worsened the situation, strengthening nationalist and xenophobic sentiment in many countries.

The criticism aimed at Angela Merkel, even within her own party; the ire aimed at David Cameron; the growth of the National Front in France; and the groundswell of populism in Austria, Hungary, and Poland are symptoms of a weakening of European solidarity. An upshot has been a general reluctance to accept refugees, the imposition of quota systems, and the limitation of asylum grants to ridiculously small, inhumane numbers.

All this calls into question not simply the well-being of thousands of people, but also European identity if the Union is incapable of working through the crisis and changing its values accordingly.

With reference to the 1948 Universal Declaration of Human Rights, the question the migrant crisis puts before us is likely not so much whether one must take in those vulnerable parties compelled by necessity to emigrate but how to do it. Drawing on Ortega's distinction between the urgent and the important, we aver that what is important is creating a cosmopolitan society in which all human beings can feel themselves to be citizens. This society has its roots in the dream of the Stoics, who knew themselves to be citizens of their country but also citizens of the world. This continued through Christianity, was crystallized in the Enlightenment, and remains one of the great challenges for our time.

Crucial to this tradition is the value of hospitality, at once a virtue, an attitude, and a duty corresponding to a right that impends upon judicial, political, and social institutions as well as the state itself. There is an unconditional obligation to hospitality that is anterior to the duty and right but that is necessarily realized through them. If, as Kant says, intuitions without categories are blind and categories without intuitions are empty, we may say that without laws and political action, the unconditional

obligation to hospitality is empty; but without that unconditional obligation, asylum and immigration policy are blind. This
is the dialectic we find ourselves in and we must confront it
head-on, because if Europe wishes to maintain its identity, it
must reinforce this obligation to hospitality that was born on
its soil, understood not just as domestic hospitality, but also as
institutional and universal.

A Sign of Civilization

The term "hospitality" retains the sense of the Greek *filoxenia,*
love or affection for strangers, and is derived from the Latin
hospitare, "to receive as a guest." It is kindness on the part of one
who gives shelter to visitors and strangers. Traditionally, it has
been associated with pilgrims, beggars, and the disadvantaged,
who are aided in times of need. It is synonymous with shelter,
asylum, acceptance, and protection; its opposites are rejection
and hostility.

Domestic hospitality, the willingness to take in strangers,
was an everyday virtue in the ancient world in the East as well
as in the West. It needed no justification: taking in strangers and
the needy was a sign of civility or religion, and was not open to
question. Rejecting a stranger in need of aid demanded a justification, because societies took the obligation to shelter as a
matter of course.

The Western tradition abounds with tales of hospitality, in
which the stranger in need of food or shelter was often a divin-
ity in disguise, from the Iliad and Odyssey to the myth of Phi-
lemon and Baucis, in which Zeus and Hermes seek asylum in
Tyana, and save the couple that takes them in from a flood that
destroys the city. In Genesis, Abraham and Sara learn that they
will have a child thanks to three pilgrims whom they give food,

water, and shelter from the sun. It is impossible to tell from the verses whether one of them is Yahweh, but there is no doubt that they receive the good news thanks to Abraham's hospitality and in spite of Sara's distrust.[2] And Saint Paul writes in Hebrews: "Be not forgetful to entertain strangers: for thereby some have entertained angels unawares."[3]

Throughout the Old Testament, Yahweh stresses to the Israelites the duty of hospitality, reminding them that they too were strangers in Egypt.[4] And the New Testament prizes hospitality as one of the traits that the Son of Man will consider with regard to salvation: "I was a stranger, and ye took me in."[5] The stranger is sacred, and sheltering him is the proper response.

In all these cases, hospitality is a personal virtue, but also a duty that brings to light the stranger's need and vulnerability. It is a response to helplessness—the only human response.

Hospitality at the individual level is indispensable to respond to the massive exodus produced by hunger and war and others sure to come as desertification sweeps the planet and leaves fewer and fewer people with access to water. And it is praiseworthy that families have taken in people from elsewhere without waiting for institutions to take the lead. But this is insufficient: we also need an institutionalization of hospitality that removes it from the hands of individuals alone. Just as Luis Vives felt poverty demanded the involvement of municipal governments, mass immigration also demands institutional solutions.[6]

A Virtue of Life in Common

Immanuel Kant offered two definitions of hospitality that are linked but differ a great deal from each other. The first describes it as a necessary virtue for life in common; the second, as a right and a duty. Both have significance for the present, the second perhaps more than the first. Kant examined these matters in his *Lectures on Ethics*, but his main discussion of them appears in Section 48 of the *Metaphysics of Morals*.[7] The social virtues here lack much of their original ethical significance and the religious trappings of the concept of hospitality, and instead become virtues for life in common. Kant states that the social virtues are not virtues as such, because "they are not addressed to need, but merely to comfort, and there is no more to them than the pleasures and amenities of people in company."[8]

Kant is ambiguous here. He justifies the social virtues as virtues by saying that every person is the center of himself, but must relate with others, with the circle of his actions extending outward to its furthest reaches in cosmopolitan society.[9] And yet he expressly says that they are not virtues, because they do not strengthen the soul for the fulfillment of duty, instead facilitating life in common and making virtue more pleasant and attractive.

The social virtues attempt to foment reciprocal communication, amenity, the spirit of conciliation, and mutual love and respect, affability, and decorum—all that Kant calls *humanitas aesthetica*. He states that the social virtues possess great civilizing force, because we need courtesy and kind treatment from others. But from the moral point of view, Kant calls them external adornments, "small coin" that deceives nobody.

He adds that the social virtues favor the feeling of virtue because affability, an expansive character, courtesy, hospitality, and the goodwill of the person who knows how to demure without argumentation, come as close to virtue as possible without actually partaking of it.[10] They humanize and civilize, thus preparing man to experience the moral force of the true virtues.[11] They are manners, but they create obligations and exert influence in favor of virtuous intentions by making them the object of general esteem.[12]

It is difficult not to recall, when reading these texts, that the codes of ethics of tourism place immense value on hospitality, the virtue of life in common that makes it agreeable, satisfying the needs of the guest, which admittedly are not essential, and can be reduced to the desire for kind treatment. This desire has even given rise to a branch of study known as "hospitality sciences," with degree programs and academic research devoted to it. These prove that greater attention on the part of the host toward the guest's desires may raise profits greater than a single-minded focus on profits alone.

Returning to Kant, the notion of the individual as embedded in a series of concentric circles, the widest of which is the cosmopolitan, may suffuse hospitality with a more rigorous moral character, pointing the way toward a society without exclusion. Still, the personal virtues of life in common are insufficient to develop a humane approach to the problem of massive displacements of the needy. What is required is that feeling of open hospitality so prized in the Biblical, Greek, and Roman worlds, but modified to fit with the demands of cosmopolitan society. Doing this demands reexamining the second concept of hospitality put forward by Kant, that of Cosmopolitan Law, which allows us to bridge personal virtue and the institutional obligation to offer shelter to foreigners. This enshrines personal virtue as a legal duty corresponding to the right of the foreigner to be accommodated.

Hospitality as a Right and Duty

Kant examines hospitality as a legal duty in his attempts to sketch out Cosmopolitan Law in *Perpetual Peace* and in the Doctrine of Right in *The Metaphysics of Morals*. Lasting peace, he writes, cannot exist without eliminating the causes of war, and this can only be achieved in a cosmopolitan society in which all people are recognized without exception as citizens. To this end, Cosmopolitan Law must impose conditions of universal hospitality. This is not philanthropy, but a legal duty that corresponds to a legal right.

Cosmopolitanism has not always been seen in a positive light. Massimo Mori recalls that such texts as Louis-Charles Fougeret de Montbron's *Le cosmopolite, ou Le citoyen du monde* take the cosmopolitan to be a radical individualist who rejects all commitment to the community in favor of his own personal interest. He adds the following highly expressive excerpt from this text: "All countries are the same to me, so long as I enjoy the clear skies and may conserve my individuality until the end. Absolute master of my will and absolutely independent, changing dwellings, customs, and climes at will, I cling to everything and nothing."[13] The 1762 *Dictionnaire de l'Académie française* states: "The cosmopolitan is not a good citizen." Rousseau inveighs similarly against "those cosmopolitans who go to great lengths in their books to discover duties they do not deign to fulfill around them."[14]

But in that same century, a positive view of cosmopolitanism began to gather strength among authors like Voltaire, Shaftesbury, Lessing, and Kant. The cosmopolitanism favored here is cultural; Kant's decisive contribution was his conviction that it implied a juridical problem that could not be resolved without defining the relations between man and state in legal terms.[15] But the Kantian view has limitations, because law alone is not enough: ethics and politics must be drawn in, too.

Turning to *Perpetual Peace*, a 1795 work dealing with the possibility of lasting peace among human beings, we must note that Kant's preface begins ironically, describing the book's title as taken from the signboard of a Dutch innkeeper.[16] Nonetheless, the work contains ideas that ought not be put aside blithely.[17] As is well known, Kant's vision of the state of nature is a pessimistic one, closely linked to Hobbes, and he believes it a moral duty to emerge from the state of permanent war in which human beings cannot develop their autonomy or organize peaceful life in common.[18] For this reason, the drafting of a pact creating a political community, the state, is a moral duty. But this pact cannot conduce only to contingent peace; perpetual peace is not a utopia, but a regulatory idea. This means that even if, from a theoretical point of view, the possibility of perpetual peace cannot be affirmed or negated, from the practical perspective, working toward it is a moral obligation, because practical reason dictates that war should not exist as it is unsuited to each person attaining his rights.[19] This echoes the following from Hobbes:

> For war consisteth not in battle only, or the act of fighting, but in a tract of time, wherein the will to contend by battle is sufficiently known: and therefore the notion of time is to be considered in the nature of war, as it is in the nature of weather. For as the nature of foul weather lieth not in a shower or two of rain, but in an inclination thereto of many days together: so the nature of war consisteth not in actual fighting, but in the known disposition thereto during all the time there is no assurance to the contrary. All other time is peace.[20]

It is thus impossible to speak of peace while people find themselves in a situation of potential war: there must exist a guarantee that the desire to fight has abated. Hobbes believes this guarantee can be found in the pact that turns absolute power over to the sovereign. Kant, on the other hand, proposes six preliminary and three definitive articles for perpetual peace.

The three definitive articles are as follows: "The Civil Constitution in every State shall be Republican"; "The Right of Nations shall be founded on a Federation of Free States"; and "The Rights of men as Citizens of the world in a cosmo-political system, shall be restricted to conditions of universal Hospitality."[21] Peace is not to be assured through armaments conceived for preventive war, but in the republicanization of all states, the establishment of relations between them, and the aspiration to a cosmopolitan society.

In Kantian philosophy, the ideas of perpetual peace and cosmopolitanism are closely linked, and peace is one of the attractions of cosmopolitanism. This is a debatable point, because aspiring to a cosmopolitan society in the *Lectures on Ethics* and other works is put forward as a regulative idea and hence valuable in itself. At any rate, the third article quoted above is the one that interests us most as regards the concept of hospitality. With it is born an idea of hospitality that refers not solely to interpersonal relations, that is not a virtue of civility or life in common, that is indeed a duty of states and their inhabitants. This enigmatic conception contains the keys of cosmopolitan law. So what does it consist of?

To lay the groundwork, we must recall that two interpretations of Kantian cosmopolitanism have been put forward that continue to be relevant today.[22] According to the first, cosmopolitanism will be achieved when all states have become republics and have joined their wills in a federation of free states as specified in the second article of *Perpetual Peace*. The second conceives of cosmopolitan society as a world state. This would be the outcome of Cosmopolitan Law as outlined in the Doctrine of Right in *The Metaphysics of Morals*, which confers upon individuals the status of citizens of the world.

Support for the second hypothesis can be found in texts of Kant's from 1793 and 1795 as well as in Section 83 of the *Critique of Judgment*, which affirms that the end of culture is the formation of a "cosmopolitan whole." What seems improbable here is that cosmopolitan law speaks not of a world state in which all people are recognized as citizens, but rather the right of citizens to be treated with hospitality when they go peacefully into other countries and the duty of the inhabitants of those countries not to reject them so long as they fulfill certain conditions.[23] This leads one to presume that the states are different rather than parts of a world state.

He is speaking of the *right* of those who travel to foreign lands precisely because his intent is to sketch out a cosmopolitan law, not to propose philanthropic suggestions. The person who arrives in a foreign land has a right to be treated with hospitality rather than with hostility for the mere fact of his foreign origin. It is difficult here not to pivot to the present moment and insist that refugees and immigrants have a right to be taken in with hospitality, and that those who live in their countries of arrival are not entitled to reject them with hostility. A fine point must be added here: the inhabitant of a country may reject a foreigner if he does not severely injure him by doing so.

But what if this rejection does lead to harm or death for the other? We find no answer in Kant because our era is not comparable with his: no great quantity of immigrants struggling to survive was arriving to Kant's hometown of Königsberg or anywhere else in Europe at the end of the eighteenth century. Kant was thinking rather of conquistadors who barge into foreign lands to trade and colonize. That is why he speaks of the right to visit rather than the right to be taken in. This is a crucial difference.

The right of resort states that "All men are entitled to present themselves thus to society in virtue of their right to the common possession of the surface of the earth,[24] to no part of which anyone had originally more right than another; and upon which, from its being a globe, they cannot scatter themselves to infinite distances, but must at last bear to live side by side with each other."[25]

The second of these propositions in fact depends on the first. If the earth is possessed in common, and no one has more right than any other to be in a given place, then the person whose life conditions are poor where fortune has placed him or the person who wishes to prosper elsewhere both have a right to depart. They may look for uninhabited lands, but given the finitude of the earth, the natural thing is that they encounter other inhabitants of it who ought not treat them with hostility so long as they come in peace because their claim has no more status than that of anyone else.

Each person's birthplace is contingent, and so everyone has a right to go to a place different from where he was born. Kant says as much in *The Metaphysics of Morals*:

> All men are originally (i.e., prior to any act of choice that establishes a right) in a possession of land that is in conformity with right, that is, they have a right to be wherever nature or chance (apart from their will) has placed them.[26]

All people, then, possess a natural right to take possession of a place on the non-infinite, spherical surface of the earth. In the ancient tradition of *ius naturalis*, the common ownership of earth is a gift of God, and this is a presupposition that runs like a thread through the Doctrine of Right following a route marked out by nature or providence through to Constitutional Law, International Law, and Cosmopolitan Law.[27] A hospitable society, along with recognition of human dignity, is essential. Why, then, is there a right of entry, but not a right to hospitality?

The right to hospitality demands a contract in which the foreigner is permitted to remain for a period of time in the new land. In the eighteenth century, this limitation and the demand for a contractual basis was a defense of the weak and vulnerable, curbing the right of colonizers to occupy other lands, establishing that the legal maximum that Europeans were entitled to was a right to resort and placing the issuance of this entitlement in the hands of the poor nations.[28]

Kant's proposal concerning hospitality is a great step forward because, by insisting on the duty to suppress hostility toward the visitor to another country, it opens the path to a universal community. As he affirms of kind treatment "In this way distant parts of the world can enter peaceably into relations with one another, which eventually become publicly lawful and so finally bring the human race even closer to a cosmopolitical constitution."[29]

A cosmopolitan constitution is not an impossible idea, neither "high flown nor exaggerated." First because advances have been made in the establishment of a community among all the peoples of the earth, so that violations in one place have repercussions elsewhere. Cosmopolitan Law is necessary to embody the unwritten code of Contractual Law for humanity, complementing the explicit canons of Contractual Law and International Law and comprising a condition for approaching perpetual peace.

Many questions arise around this notion of the right to hospitality, particularly if one attempts to apply it to the twenty-first century. Kant derives his bases for the right to be taken in during times of need in at least two principles: the defense of personal dignity and the primordial ownership of the earth. But as Vlachos writes, pragmatism often demands curtailing the uncompromising impulse of ethics in the political realm.[30] Then again, such failures as that of the States General in The Hague suggest that a federation of independent states is highly improbable, and the dream of a world state Kant presumes would necessarily tend to despotism. So long as there are different states, they are required to protect their citizens while also allowing visits from those who come peacefully from without, particularly if rejecting them were to lead to harm.

But states' disposition to curtail the unconditional hospitality that morality demands leads to problems that twentieth-century philosophers like Lévinas and Derrida have attempted to address, critiquing the errors of neoliberal individualism through the assertion that openness to the other is a basic characteristic of humanity. This openness naturally includes the demand to take in those in need. The absolute, infinite law of hospitality transcends pacts and contracts and demands opening the political realm to whoever needs it; and ethical demands precede obligations and laws.

Shelter: An Unconditional Ethical Demand

Though Lévinas does not employ frequently the term "hospitality," his idea of openness to the other, of taking the other in, has inspired others to do so.[31] Openness, according to Lévinas, does not mean taking the stranger into one's home, nation, or city, but being open to him; this openness or welcoming of the alterity of the other is constitutive of our nature. Openness to the other is a primordial state, from which rejection and closing of doors departs. In reality, there is an a priori bond between I and another. The self is a hostage of the other.[32]

Lévinas abandons the Western tradition in which the totality takes priority over the individual and returns to the Hebrew one in which the Absolute, Yahweh, is present in the face of the other, and demands responsibility for him. European civilization, Lévinas writes, opened a schism between others and us through the construction of cities, which generated a mass of the excluded. From the security of the *oikos*, the home, the occident tends toward construction and settlement and is terrified of pilgrimage and nomadism. Against this, Lévinas insists on the primacy of a humanity that is constituted above all by being with others, relating to others, having responsibility toward others. This is indeed the structure that constitutes the subject. Responsibility is not a mere attribute of a subjectivity that existed as such prior to ethical relations; it exists not for itself, but for the other.[33] This is the basis of the philosophy of hospitality, of welcoming and being welcomed.[34]

And so all types of totality and totalization are subordinated to a superior criterion that is not humanity, but rather the face of the other and his speech, which break with the absolutism of the totality. A person is not an example of a law that must be respected; instead, respect is a response to the other's face. Like Kant, Lévinas takes universal peace as a horizon to be striven toward.

Derrida follows a similar line, analyzing the ethics and politics of hospitality in light of openness and welcoming as keys for all subsequent action.[35] Derrida wishes to prolong the cosmopolitan tradition that begins with Socrates, culminates in Kant, and abides in hospitality toward strangers. Hospitality here means attention, welcoming, saying yes to the other.

This absolute duty to hospitality, in order not to be relegated to the utopian, must be embodied in law—conditioned, specifically, by the cosmopolitan law and the conditions of universal hospitality it proposes as a condition of perpetual peace.[36] In the process, limitations are placed upon it, and the duty ceases to be absolute. Paradoxically, the idea of unconditional hospitality gives meaning to the laws that place brakes upon it, and so political responsibility here necessitates mediating between broader and narrower definitions of hospitality to the end of discovering the least worst legislation possible.

The Urgent and the Important

What this means is arbitration between the ethical principle of compassionate hospitality and the conditions that embody it in countries, international organizations, and across the globe.[37] This is true for urgent cases, but also for others that are no less important for being less pressing.

What is urgent is for each country to develop mature policies with regard to asylum and integration, with quotas that take into account country size, population, the number of applications, unemployment rates, and tax bases. International institutions should be strengthened to be able to force the hands of countries reluctant to fulfill their responsibilities. And policy should be drafted with actual living persons in mind, so that they are not reduced to numbers filling internment camps or abandoned to their fate.

Anti-human-trafficking legislation is certainly essential, but the police and judiciary must be aided by improved information sharing and better cooperation with other countries. Immigration policies must be regularized to ease the extraordinary difficulties of legal immigration. Mechanisms for asylum seekers should also be streamlined so that applicants can be duly registered and those rejected may be guaranteed a proper return.

The obstacles administrations place in the way of citizen organizations that attempt to aid displaced persons must be cleared away. The exercise of the private virtue of hospitality cannot be prohibited.

There must be greater economic commitments made to immigrants and refugees, whether this means raising taxes or generating funds through other means. Solidarity cannot exist without economic collaboration.

As far as longer-term goals, international organizations like the EU and the UN must work to create peace by every means available in the countries that are sources of refugees, like Syria, where more than half the residents have been displaced and more than two hundred and fifty thousand people have died. Irrespective of fractures in the EU and the divisions in America that have become evident since the Trump election, achieving peace is a challenge that must be met.

We must also adopt the UN's 2030 agenda to build a cosmopolitan society, whether through global governance, a democratic world state, or a federation. And the key to it must be universal hospitality, which will follow the dictates of justice and make the world a home for all human beings.

Cosmopolitan Hospitality: Justice and Compassion

Returning to Lévinas: his attack on the centrality of the city and settlement in the Western tradition as a basis of the distinction between us and them appears dubious in the light of what we have seen in earlier chapters with regard to hunter-gatherers and the us-them distinctions that reinforce their protective bonds in the small group setting, all of which dates back to long before the Greek culture of the *oikos* and entered the brain millennia before the dawn of Western civilization. It is instead a biocultural code of conduct that is part of *homo sapiens* and cannot be ascribed simplistically to one civilization or another.

People are born in relation, in bonds, not as isolated individuals or atoms closed in on themselves. They have survived thanks to their solidarity with their neighbors and their self-defense before outsiders: that is the key to the xenophobic brain. Slowly they learned to practice cooperation and reciprocal exchange with others who possessed benefits, forming thereby a new category of *us* based on mutual benefit to the detriment of the *aporoi* who seemed disqualified from entering into this game: that is the key to aporophobia and the aporophobic brain. Though our present environments have changed a great deal compared to primitive societies, the human species has remained essentially the same as it was forty thousand years ago, following a morality rooted in groups seeking mutual benefit. Moral progress isn't heritable; every person must learn it by living alongside others who help along the way.

Fortunately, the brain is highly plastic and can cultivate openness to the other, to any and all others, through compassionate recognition, which is the essence of universal hospitality.

This is not to merely affirm, with Kant, that all people have the right to travel to all places on earth or that vulnerable lands cannot be invaded. And it is also something more than the mere affirmation of openness upon seeing the face of the other—as though hospitality depended on the other and not on us.

Unconditional ethics arises from the recognition of dignity, respect for one's own dignity and the dignity of others. But it is also anchored in solidarity with those in vulnerable situations. True, all people are vulnerable, but some need more help than others, depending on their place in time, to enjoy a good life or even simply to live.[38] The only humane ethical and political response in these cases is universal hospitality, which should orient the very nature of judicial and political institutions.

This is truer still when recognition goes beyond that dignity that all human beings are entitled to and beyond solidarity with the needy to encompass the cordial recognition that our lives are primordially linked and must be carried out with compassion.[39]

An ethics of co-responsibility demands that present-day policy and law be exercised from a base of compassionate recognition oriented toward the construction of a nonexclusionary cosmopolitan society. This is an unavoidable challenge for education, which must begin with the family and school and continue in the different areas of public life.

A system of education suitable for the twenty-first century is obliged to produce citizens open to the world, but also capable of grasping the challenges of their place and time; people sensitive to all that remains to be overcome, from the refugee crisis to extreme poverty, hunger, the defenselessness of the vulnerable, millions of premature deaths, and neglected illnesses. Educating for our time means shaping compassionate citizens who cannot only adopt the perspectives of those who suffer, but can also commit to helping them.

Notes

Chapter 1. A Scourge without a Name

1. García Márquez, 1969, 1.
2. Zweig, 1953, 209.
3. Cortina, 2013.

Chapter 2. Hate Crimes against the Poor

1. Glucksmann, 2005, 96.
2. *Informe sobre incidentes relacionados con los delitos de odio en España, 2014.* Ministerio del Interior, 2015, 3.
3. Chakraborti, Garland, and Hardy, 2014.
4. The seventh recommendation of the European Commission Against Racism and Intolerance (ECRI) (2007) identifies hate speech as deliberate expressions that imply a public incitement to violence, hatred, or discrimination, as well as insults and defamation based on race, color, language, religion, nationality, or ethnicity; section IV of this document recommends its penalization under criminal law.

The European Tribunal on Human Rights defines hate speech in the same way in Recommendation 20 of the Committee of Ministers of the Council of Europe (1997) as "all ideologies, policies and practices constituting an incitement to racial hatred, violence and discrimination, as well as any action or language likely to strengthen fears and tensions between groups from different racial, ethnic, national, religious or social backgrounds" (Rey, 2015, 53, note 4).

5. Observatorio Hatento, 2015a, 29.
6. Cortina, 2000b.
7. These three characteristics are taken from Parekh, 2006, according to whom hate speech (1) is directed against a particular group of people, whether Muslims, Jews, indigents, homosexual people, or others; (2) stigmatizes this group with negative stereotypes; and (3) intends these alleged characteristics to justify these groups' exclusion from society and contempt and hostility aimed at them.

8. Chakraborti, 2011.

9. Cortina, 1986, chap. 6; 2001, chap. 9.

10. Observatorio Hatento, 2015b, 38.

11. Tercer *Informe sobre los Delitos de Odio*, 2015, 62.

12. Observatorio Hatento, 2015b, 16.

13. Ibid.

Chapter 3. Hate Speech

1. This chapter developed from a lecture delivered at the first workshop of the research project "Protection of Minorities in the Face of Hate Speech," directed by Juan A. Carrillo and Pedro Rivas, at Loyola University in Andalusia in Seville on October 6, 2016, and from my lecture at a reunion of the Royal Academy of Moral and Political Sciences on November 25, 2016.

2. Title I: "Fundamental Rights and Duties." The International Covenant on Civil and Political Rights, article 19.3 affirms that restrictions on freedom of expression must be expressly codified in law and may only exist in order to: (a) assure respect for the rights and reputation of others; (b) protect national security, public order, or moral and public health. Article 10.2 of the European Convention on Human Rights of 1950 mentions "the interests of national security, territorial integrity or public safety, for the prevention of disorder or crime, for the protection of health or morals, for the protection of the reputation or rights of others, for preventing the disclosure of information received in confidence, or for maintaining the authority and impartiality of the judiciary."

3. Observatorio Hatento, 2015a, 29.

4. For the importance of viewing hate speech within the framework of antidiscrimination law, see Rey, 2015; Carrillo, in publication.

5. Carrillo, 2015, 208–11.

6. Highly illuminating here is Santiago Muñoz Machado's speech, given upon his acceptance into the Royal Spanish Academy of Language, on *The Itineraries of Freedom of Speech* (Muñoz Machado, 2013).

7. Rey, 2015, 49ff.

8. Rawls, 1996, 85–89; Martínez-Torrón, 2016, 29.

9. See, for example, Hare and Weinstein, 2010.

10. Rey, 2015a.

11. Ibid.; Carrillo, in publication.

12. Revenga, 2015b. Though the American and European positions have gradually begun to converge, we will consider the first two models as ideal types in the Weberian sense.

13. As Muñoz Machado and others have shown, freedom of speech appears initially as parliamentary freedom, which should protect the members of chambers from responsibility for opinions aired in debates. Thomas More was the first to propose it to King Henry VIII in 1521. Questions about how to control it arise with its application to the printing press (Muñoz Machado, 2013, chap. 4). In North America, debate has followed the parameters laid out by Locke, Trenchard, and Gordon (see ibid., chap. 5).

14. For the evolution of freedom of speech in the United States from 1952 to 1978, see Walker, 1994, chap. 6.

15. The Spanish Supreme Court, in STC 174/2006, FJ 4 affirms that "freedom of expression encompasses the freedom to criticize, even when this is extreme and may cause irritation, grievance, or displeasure in its object, because this is a demand of the pluralism, tolerance, and spirit of openness without which democratic societies cannot exist" (Revenga, 2015b, 24, note 20).

16. Loewenstein, 1937a and b.

17. Barber, 2004; Cortina, 1993, 102–7.

18. John Milton, 1611.

19. Constant, 1989.

20. Revenga, 2015b, 30.

21. Kant, 1991, 15.

22. Ibid., 40.

23. Hegel, 1975, section 33.

24. Conill, 2004; Conill and Gozálvez, 2004; Cortina, 1993; Cortina and García-Marzá, 2003; García-Marzá, 2004; Gracia, 1989; Lozano, 2004; Martínez Navarro, 2000.

25. Cortina, 1993.

26. Apel, 1998; Habermas, 1990.

27. Cortina, 2007.

28. Austin, 1975; Searle, 1970.

29. Apel, 1985; Habermas, 1985; Conill, 2006; Cortina, 2007; Honneth, 1996; Ricœur, 2005; Siurana, 2003.

30. Apel, 1980, 299.

31. General Recommendation 35 of the United Nations Committee on the Elimination of Racial Discrimination, approved in August of 2013, states: "The relationship between proscription of racist hate speech and the flourishing of freedom of expression should be seen as complementary and not the expression of a zero sum game where the priority given to one necessitates the diminution of the other." (Rey, 2015a, 86). Without a civic ethics drafted along these lines, this is impossible.

Chapter 4. Our Brain Is Aporophobic

1. Eagleman, 2012, 224.

2. Sen, 2001; Conill, 2004.

3. Conill, 2004.

4. Cortina, 1986, 2001.

5. Taylor, 1994.

6. Marshall and Bottomore, 1987.

7. Cortina, 1997; Pogge, 2008.

8. Cortina, 1997; Pogge, 2008.

9. Kohlberg, 1981.

10. Aranguren, 1994.

11. Ovid, *Metamorphoses*, Book VII.

12. Saint Paul, Epistle to Romans, 7:19.

13. Cortina, 2011 and 2012.

14. Amor Pan, 2015, 23–27; Blanco, 2014.

15. Amor Pan, 2015, 53.

16. Amor Pan, 2015, 43–45.

17. Choudury et al., 2009; Choudury and Slaby, 2011; García-Marzá, 2012.

18. Churchland, 2011, 3; Suhler and Churchland, 2011, 33.

19. Changeux, 1985 and 2010; Edelman and Tononi, 2000; Evers, 2010 and 2015; Fuster, 2014.

20. Eagleman, 2013, 131–34.

21. Eagleman, 2013, 182.

22. Evers, 2015, 1, 2.

23. Edelman, 1992.

24. Evers, 2015, 4.

25. Damasio, 2011, 51, 52.

26. Churchland, 2011, 14.

27. Churchland, 2011; Cortina, 2011; Damasio, 2011; Evers, 2010 and 2015; Haidt, 2012b; Hauser, 2009; Levy, 2007.

28. Evers, 2015, 4.

29. Rizzolatti and Sinigaglia, 2006; Iacoboni, 2008.

30. Smith, 1759; Sen, 1977, 2002, 35–37.

31. Evers, 2015, 5.

32. Wilson, 1993.

33. See Greene, 2012; Gazzaniga, 2009, 172, 173.

34. Greene, 2012; Gazzaniga, 2009, 172, 173.

35. Darwin, 1871.

36. Hauser, 2009, chap. 7; Cortina, 2011, chap. 4; 2012, 9–38.

37. Hamilton, 1964a, 1964b.

38. Nowak and Sigmund, 2000, 819; Conill, 2012.

39. Kant, 2006.

40. Codina, 2015.

41. Lewontin, Rose and Kamin, 2017.

42. Cortina, 2007, 125.

Chapter 5. Conscience and Reputation

1. Fuentes, 2003, p. 10. These words have their origin in a lecture at the reunion of the Royal Academy of Moral and Political Sciences on March 17, 2016, and the article "Conscience and Reputation" in *El País*, August 22, 2015.

2. "Man wird mit seinem schlechten Gewissen leichter fertig, als mit seinem schlechten Rufe," Nietzsche, 1999, 416.

3. Plato, *Collected Dialogues*.

4. Moll, 2002, 2730; 2005, 807.

5. Haidt, 2012b, 220.

6. Ibid.

7. Robert Audi offers a good definition of naturalism: "In very broad terms, we might think of it as the position that, first, nature—conceived as the physical universe—is all there is; second, the only basic truths are truths of nature; and, third, the only substantive knowledge is of natural facts" (Audi, 2013, 2). For the debate on ethical naturalism, see Nuccetelli and Shea, 2012; Joyce, 2014; Kitcher, 2014; Ortega, 2016.

8. Darwin, 1871.

9. Waal, 2014.

10. Darwin, 1871.

11. See Richart, 2016.

12. For a compilation of evolutionary perspectives on consciousness, see F. B. M. de Waal, P. S. Churchland, T. Pievani, and S. Parmigiani, eds., 2014.

13. "With mankind, selfishness, experience, and imitation, probably add, as Mr. Bain has shewn, to the power of sympathy; for we are led by the hope of receiving good in return to perform acts of sympathetic kindness to others; and sympathy is much strengthened by habit. In however complex a manner this feeling may have originated, as it is one of high importance to all those animals which aid and defend one another, it will have been increased through natural selection; for those communities, which included the greatest number of the most sympathetic members, would flourish best, and rear the greatest number of offspring" (Darwin, 1871).

14. Trivers, 1971.

15. The belief that we internalize social rules and that altruistic conduct eventuates is shared by Simon, 1990, and Gintis, 2003.

16. Alexander, 1987.

17. Boehm, 2012, 14.

18. Darwin, 1871.

19. If this is the case, then Hume was right to affirm that pride and the feeling of inferiority are natural passions original to man and linked to the feeling of sympathy. Individuals feel proud when they contemplate their virtue, wealth, and power, and this impression of pride is agreeable, while the feeling of inferiority gives rise to the opposite impression. We live through others' opinion and thus "We fancy Ourselves more happy, as well as more virtuous or beautiful, when we appear so to others; but are still more ostentatious of our virtues than of our pleasures. This proceeds from causes, which I shall endeavour to explain afterwards" (Hume, 1739). If the most basic human feelings are the agreeable and the disagreeable, then pride is agreeable and inferiority disagreeable, and this is essential to understanding our moral lives.

20. Boehm, 2012, chap. 6.

21. Alexander, 1987, 102.

22. Boehm, 2012, 113.

23. Churchland, 2011, 192. Elsewhere, she states, "Morality seems to me to be a natural phenomenon—constrained by the forces of natural selection, rooted in neurobiology, shaped by the local ecology, and modified by cultural development."

24. Boehm, 2012, 32; Rawls, 1971, section 67. For the neuronal bases of reputation-based decision-making, see Izuma, 2012.

25. Nowak and Sigmund, 2000.

26. Alexander, 1987.

27. Axelrod, 1984.

28. Wedekind and Milinski, 2000; Seinen and Schram, 2006; Engelmann and Fischbacher, 2009; Ito, Fujii, Ueno, Koseki, Tashiro, and Mori, 2010–2011; Izuma, 2012.

29. Ernst Fehr and Frédéric Schneider, however, propose a different position with regard to eye signaling and altruistic or prosocial conduct. See Fehr and Schneider, 2010.

30. Bergson, 1977.

31. Darwin, 1871.

32. "The other so-called self-regarding virtues, which do not obviously, though they may really, affect the welfare of the tribe, have never been esteemed by savages, though now highly appreciated by civilised nations" (Darwin, 1871).

33. Contradictory as it may seem, he declares openly, "For I can recognize that I am under obligation to others only insofar as I at the same time put myself under obligation, since the law by virtue of which I regard myself as being under obligation proceeds in every case from my own practical reason; and in being constrained by my own reason, I am also the one constraining myself" (Kant 1991, 214).

34. Kant, 2012; Cortina, 2007, 2011, and 2013.

Chapter 6. Moral Bioenhancement

1. This chapter originated with the article "¿Es la biomejora moral un imperativo ético?," in *Sistema*, no. 230 (2013): 3–14, and with "Neuromejora moral: ¿un camino prometedor ante el fracaso de la educación?," in *Anales de la Real Academia de Ciencias Morales y Políticas*, no. 90 (2013): 313–31.

2. Harris, 2009.

3. Safire, 2002, 3–9; Cortina, 2011, 36–39.

4. Buchanan, 2011, 23.

5. Savulescu, 2012, 313, 314.

6. Savulescu and Bostrom, 2009, 1–24.

7. Bostrom, 2005.

8. Huxley, quoted in Hughes, 2004.

9. Douglas, 2008, 228. Douglas recognizes that some authors are selective and not opposed to enhancements of all kinds (ibid., 243, note 7).

10. Sandel, 2007; Fukuyama, 2002.

11. Buchanan, 2011, 13.

12. Allen Buchanan proposes initiating an *enhancement enterprise* that follows humanity's self-improving mission, building a society that frees individuals and organizations to develop enhancement technologies, devoting public resources to research and opening a public and informed debate about the subject aimed at developing morally viable politics around it.

13. Sandel, 2007, 89–92.

14. Douglas, 2008, 229.

15. Ibid., 233.

16. Savulescu and Persson, 2012.

17. Savulescu and Persson, 2012.

18. Apel, 1985, 342.

19. Jonas, 1994.

20. Cela and Ayala, 2001, chap. 11; Cortina, 2011, chap. 4.

21. Tomasello, 2009.

22. Savulescu, 2012, 231.

23. Hamilton, 1964a, 1964b; Axelrod and Hamilton, 1981; Axelrod 1984; Skyrms, 1996; Nowak and Sigmund, 2000, 819; Levy, 2007; Hauser, 2009, 340; Tomasello, 2010, and Cortina, 2011.

24. Conill, 2012; Kahneman, 2011.

25. If human rationality truly signified maximizing benefits, in this game, a rational respondent would accept any offer greater than zero, and the rational proposer would offer the closest quantity to zero to gain more. But respondents tend to reject offers of less than 30 percent, preferring nothing to a humiliating offer; and for this

reason, proposers tend to offer 40 percent to 50 percent of the total to be able to retain something (Nowak et al., 2000). Similar to this is the game of dictator.

26. Jensen, Call, and Tomasello, 2007, 107–9; Tomasello, 2010, 56, 57.

27. Hume, 1739.

28. Kant, 1991, 245-46

29. Marcus, 2002; Krause, 2008.

30. Savulescu, 2012, 216.

31. Morgado, 2010.

32. Cortina, 2011, chap. 9.

33. Haidt, 2012a, 2012b; Cortina, 2011, 61–65.

34. Haidt, 2012b, 220.

35. Ibid., 201. Patricia Churchland sees oxytocin as one of the bases of morality, which is rooted in care. See Churchland, 2011.

36. Cortina, 2007; Codina, 2015; Pires, 2015.

37. Savulescu, 2012, 240, 241.

38. Agar, 1999; Habermas, 2003.

39. Kant, 1991, 250–51.

Chapter 7. Eradicating Poverty, Reducing Inequality

1. Smith, 1759.

2. Smith, 1776.

3. Tortosa, 2002, 282.

4. Sachs, 2006; Conill, 2009b.

5. Sen, 1985; Cortina and Pereira, 2009, 17–19.

6. Sachs, 2005, 51–55.

7. Sen, 2001.

8. Aristotle, 2108, 20.

9. Streeten, et al. 1981.

10. Ravallion, 2016, 9.

11. Cortina and Conill, 2016.

12. Seneca, https://en.wikisource.org/wiki/Moral_letters_to_Lucilius.

13. Seneca, https://en.wikisource.org/wiki/Moral_letters_to_Lucilius.

14. Cortina, 2002.

15. Ravallion, 2016.

16. For the history of thinking about poverty, see Morell, 2002.

17. Ravallion, 2016, 593, 594, *passim*.

18. Kant, 2102, 84.

19. Drèze and Sen, 1989; Ravallion, 2016, 29.

20. Ravallion, 2016, 4.

21. Aristotle, 1981, VI, chap. 11.

22. Aristotle, 1981, I, chap. 6.

23. Vives, 2006, 173.

24. Ibid., 174.

25. Muñoz Machado, 2013, 25.

26. Ravallion, 2016, 593.

27. Iglesias, 2008, 141.

28. Ibid., 140.

29. Habermas, 2018, 57; Walzer, 1993.

30. García Roca, 2016 and 1998.

31. Renaut, 1993.

32. Sen, 2004.

33. Gómez-Bezares, 2001; Ansotegui, Gómez-Bezares, and González Fabre, 2014.

34. Lamo de Espinosa, 2014, 35. Sachs, 2015.

35. Sachs, 2015.

36. Iglesias, 2008.

37. Novales, 2015, 1.

38. Piketty, 2017.

39. Novales, 2015, 1, 2.

40. Terceiro, 2016.

41. Crocker, 2008.

42. Van Parijs, 1995; Raventós, 1999 and 2001; Pinilla, 2004 and 2006, 45; Novales, 2015, 2.

43. Novales, 2015, 2.

44. Escudero, 2005; Sachs, 2015.

45. Ruggie, 2013; García-Marzá, 2009.

46. García-Marzá, 2004.

47. Vives, 2010.

48. Conill, 2004.

49. Zamagni, 2014, 223.

50. Moreno, 2014.

51. Ibid., 294.

52. García Delgado, Triguero, and Jiménez, 2014.

53. Smith, 1776.

54. Pope Francis, 2015.

55. Conill, 2012.

56. Cortina, 2001, 2007, and 2013.

Chapter 8. Cosmopolitan Hospitality

1. Kant, 2006, 29ff. This chapter originated in a conference at the Center of Political and Constitutional Studies on October 8, 2015, and in the article "Hospitalidad cosmopolita," published in *El País*, December 5, 2015.

2. Genesis 18:1–15.

3. Hebrews 13:2.

4. For study of hospitality in the Bible, see Torralba, 2004 and 2005.

5. Matthew, 25:35.

6. Vives, 2006.

7. Kant, 1991, 283–85.

8. Kant, 1997, 283.

9. Kant, 1991, 350.

10. Kant, 1991, 350 and 351.

11. Kant, 1997, 284.

12. Kant, 1991, 351.

13. Fougeret de Montbron, 1970, 30.

14. Rousseau, 1979, 36.

15. Mori, 2006, 308.

16. This minor work is part of a grouping of Kant's meditations on ethics, politics, law, and the philosophy of history that included such texts as "Idea for Universal History with a Cosmopolitan Purpose" (1784), "On the common saying: That may be correct in theory, but it is of no use in practice" (1793), *The Metaphysics of Morals* (1797) and *On Education* (1803).

17. "Whether this satirical inscription on a Dutch innkeeper's sign upon which a burial ground was painted had for its object mankind in general, or the rulers of states in particular, who are insatiable of war, or merely the philosophers who dream this sweet dream, it is not for us to decide" (Immanuel Kant, 2006).

18. Cortina, 1989, XV–XCI.

19. Kant, 1991, 195.

20. Hobbes, 1651.

21. Kant, 2006.

22. Habermas, 2015, 165–203.; Renaut and Savidan, 1999, 189–92; Cortina, 2005.

23. Renaut and Savidan, 1999, 189–92.

24. Kant, 2006; 1991, 78.

25. Kant, 2006.

26. Kant, 1991, 78.

27. Bertomeu, 2004.

28. Kant, 2006; 1991, 193; Renaut and Savidan, 1999, 197.

29. Kant, 2006.

30. Vlachos, 1962, 284, 285.

31. Lévinas, 1965 and 1995.

32. Derrida, 2001.

33. Lévinas, 1995, 90.

34. Sánchez Meca, 2006, 488.

35. Derrida and Dufourmantelle, 2000.

36. Biset, 2012, 256.

37. Cortina, 2015; Cortina and Torreblanca, 2016.

38. Cortina and Conill, 2016.

39. Cortina, 2007.

Bibliography

Agar, Nicholas. 1999. "Liberal Eugenics." In *Bioethics. An Anthology*, edited by Helga Juse and Peter Singer Blackwell, 171–81. Oxford: Oxford University Press.

Alexander, Richard D. 1987. *The Biology of Moral Systems*. New York: Aldine de Gruyter.

Amor Pan, José Ramón. 2015. *Bioética y Neurociencias*. Barcelona: Institut Borja de Bioética/Universitat Ramon Llull.

Ansotegui, Carmen, Fernando Gómez-Bezares, and Raúl González Fabre. 2014. *Ética de las finanzas*. Bilbao: Desclée de Brouwer.

Apel, Karl-Otto. 1998. *Toward a Transformation of Philosophy*. Translated by Glenn Ady and David Fisby. Milwaukee, WI: Marquette University Press.

Aranguren, José Luis. 1994. "Ética." In *Obras Completas*. Vol. 2, 159–502. Madrid: Trotta.

Aristotle. 1981. *The Politics*. Translated by Trevor J. Saunders. New York: Penguin.

———. 2018. *Rhetoric*. Translated by Robin Waterfield. New York: Oxford University Press.

Audi, Robert. 2013. *Moral Perception*. Princeton, NJ: Princeton University Press.

Austin, John L. 1975. *How to Do Things with Words*. Cambridge, MA: Harvard University Press.

Axelrod, Robert. 1984. *The Evolution of Cooperation*. New York: Basic Books.

Axelrod, Robert, and William D. Hamilton. 1981. "The Evolution of Cooperation." *Science* (211): 1390–96.

Barber, Benjamin. 2004. *Strong Democracy: Participatory Politics for a New Age*. Berkeley: University of California Press.

Bergson, Henri. 1977. *The Two Sources of Morality and Religion*. Translated by R. Ashley Audra. Notre Dame, IN: University of Notre Dame Press.

Bertomeu, María Julia. 2004. "De la apropiación privada a la adquisición común originaria del suelo. Un cambio metodológico 'menor' con consecuencias políticas revolucionarias." *Isegoría* 30: 127–34.

Biset, Emmanuel. 2007. "Jacques Derrida, entre violencia and hospitalidad." *Daimon* (40): 131–43.

Biset, Emmanuel. 2012. *Violencia, justicia and política. Una lectura de Derrida*. Córdoba: Eduvim.

Blanco, Carlos. 2014. *Historia de la Neurociencia*. Madrid: Biblioteca Nueva.

Boehm, Christophe. 2012. *Moral Origins*. New York: Basic Books.

Bostrom, Nick. 2005. "A History of Transhumanist Thought." *Journal of Evolution and Technology* 14 (1): 1–30.

Brock, Gillian. 2009. *Global Justice. A Cosmopolitan Account*. New York: Oxford University Press.

Buchanan, Allen. 2011. *Beyond Humanity?* Oxford: Oxford University Press.

Calvo, Patrici. 2016. "Reciprocidad cordial: bases éticas de la cooperación." In *Ideas and Valores* (165): 85–109.

Carrillo Donaire, Juan Antonio. 2015. "Libertad de expresión y 'discurso del odio' religioso: la construcción de la tolerancia en la era postsecular." *Revista de Fomento Social* 70 (278): 205–43.

———. In publication. "La protección de los derechos frente a los discursos del odio: del derecho represivo a las políticas públicas antidiscriminatorias." In *La protección de los derechos frente a los discursos del odio: de la protección penal a las políticas públicas*, edited by Juan Antonio Carrillo Donaire. Seville: Athenaica.

Cela, Camilo J., and Francisco Ayala. 2001. *Senderos de la evolución humana*. Madrid: Alianza.

Chakraborti, Neil. 2011. "Hate Crime Victimisation." *International Review of Victimology* 12: 1–4.

Chakraborti, Neil, John Garland, and Stevie-Jade Hardy. 2014. *The Leicester Hate Crime Project: Findings and Conclusions*. The Leicester Centre for Hate Studies, University of Leicester.

Changeux, Jean-Pierre. 1985. *Neuronal Man*. New York: Pantheon Books.

———. 2010. *Sobre lo verdadero, lo bello y el bien*. Madrid: Katz Editores.

Choudhury, S., S. K. Nagel, and J. Slaby. 2009. "Critical Neuroscience: Linking Neuroscience and Society through Critical Practice." *BioSocieties* 4 (1): 61–77.

Choudhury, S., and Slaby, 2011. *Critical Neuroscience: A Handbook of the Social and Cultural Contexts of Neuroscience*. New York: Wiley-Blackwell.

Churchland, Patricia S. 2011. *Braintrust*. Princeton, NJ: Princeton University Press.

Codina, María José. 2015. *Neuroeducación en virtudes cordiales. Cómo reconciliar lo que decimos con lo que hacemos*. Barcelona: Octaedro.

Comim, Flavio, and Martha C. Nussbaum, eds. 2014. *Capabilities, Gender, Equality: Towards Fundamental Entitlements*. New York: Cambridge University Press, 2014.

Conill, Jesús. 1991. *El enigma del animal fantástico*. Madrid: Tecnos.

———. 2004. *Horizontes de economía ética*. Madrid: Tecnos.

———. 2006. *Ética hermenéutica*. Madrid: Tecnos.

———. 2009a. "'La voz de la conciencia'. La conexión noológica de moralidad and religiosidad in Zubiri." *Isegoría* 40: 115–34.

———. 2009b. "Por una economía hermenéutica de la pobreza." In *Pobreza y libertad. Erradicar la pobreza desde el enfoque de las capacidades de Amartya Sen*, edited by Adela Cortina and Gustavo Pereira, 151–62. Madrid: Tecnos.

———. 2012. "Neuroeconomía." In *Guía Comares de Filosofía Práctica*, edited by Adela Cortina, 39–64. Granada: Comares, Granada.

Conill, Jesús, with Vicent Gozálvez. 2004. *Ética de los medios*. Barcelona: Gedisa.

Constant, Benjamin. 1989. *The Liberty of Ancients Compared with That of Moderns*. https://oll.libertyfund.org/title/constant-the-liberty-of-ancients-compared -with-that-of-moderns-1819.

Cortina, Adela. 1986. *Ética mínima. Introducción a la filosofía práctica*. Madrid: Tecnos.

———. 1989. "Estudio Preliminar" a Immanuel Kant, *La Metafísica de las Costumbres*, XV–XCI. Madrid: Tecnos.

———. 1993. *Ética aplicada and democracia radical*. Madrid: Tecnos.

———. 1995. "Aporofobia." In Creación Ética, *ABC Cultural*, December 1, 1995.

———, ed. 1996. *Ética. La vida moral y la reflexión ética*. 70, 71. Madrid: Santillana Secundaria.

———. 1997. *Ciudadanos del mundo. Hacia una teoría de la ciudadanía*. Madrid: Alianza.

———. 2000a. "Aporofobia." *El País*, March 7, 2000, 14.

———. 2000b. "Mujer, economía familiar and Estado del Bienestar." In *Dimensiones económicas y sociales de la familia*, 253–68. Fundación Argentaria, Visor.

———. 2001. *Alianza y contrato. Ética, política and religión*. Madrid: Trotta.

———. 2002. *Por una ética del consumo. La ciudadanía del consumidor en un mundo global*. Madrid: Taurus.

———. 2005. "El derecho a la guerra y la obligación de la paz." In *Filosofía y razón. Kant, 200 años*, edited by Manuel Vázquez and Román de la Calle, 25–44. Valencia: Universidad de Valencia.

———. 2007. *Ética de la razón cordial*. Oviedo: Nobel.

———. 2011. *Neuroética y neuropolítica. Sugerencias para la educación moral*. Madrid: Tecnos.

———, ed. 2012. *Guía Comares de Neurofilosofía práctica*. Granada: Comares.

———. 2013. *¿Para qué sirve realmente la ética?* Barcelona: Paidós.

———. 2015. "Hospitalidad cosmopolita." *El País*, December 5, 2015.

Cortina, Adela, and Jesús Conill. 2016. "Ethics of Vulnerability." In *Human Dignity of the Vulnerable in the Age of Rights*, edited by Aniceto Masferrer and Emilio García-Sánchez, 45–62. Switzerland: Springer International Publishing AG.

Cortina, Adela, and Domingo García-Marzá, eds. 2003. *Razón pública y éticas aplicadas. Los caminos de la razón práctica en una sociedad pluralista.* Madrid: Tecnos.

Cortina, Adela, and José Ignacio Torreblanca. 2016. "Décalogo para la crisis de los refugiados." *El País*, March 10, 2016.

Crocker, David A. 2008. *Ethics of Global Development: Agency, Capability and Deliberative Democracy.* Cambridge: Cambridge University Press.

Damasio, Antonio. 2003. *Looking for Spinoza: Joy, Sorrow, and the Feeling Brain.* New York: Harcourt.

Darwin, Charles. 1871. *The Descent of Man.* London: John Murray.

Derrida, Jacques. 2001. Entrevista en Staccato, December 19, 1997. In *¡Palabra! Instantáneas Filosóficas*, 49–56. Madrid: Trotta.

Derrida, Jacques, and Anne Dufourmantelle. 2000. *La hospitalidad.* Buenos Aires: Ediciones de la Flor.

Douglas, Thomas. 2008. "Moral Enhancement." *Journal of Applied Philosophy* 25 (3): 228–45.

Dworkin, Ronald. 2000. *Sovereign Virtue. The Theory and Practice of Equality.* Cambridge, MA: Harvard University Press.

Eagleman, David. 2012. *Incognito: The Secret Lives of the Brain.* New York: Vintage.

Edelman, Gerald M. 1992. *Bright Air, Brilliant Fire: On the Matter of the Mind.* New York: Basic Books.

Edelman, Gerald M., and Giulio Tononi. 2000. *A Universe of Consciousness: How Matter Becomes Imagination.* London: Allen Lane.

Englemann, Dirk, and Urs Fischbacher. 2009. "Indirect Reciprocity and Strategic Reputation Building in an Experimental Helping Game." *Games and Economic Behavior* 67 (2): 399–407.

Escudero, Manuel. 2005. *Homo globalis.* Madrid: Espasa.

Evans, Jonathan St. B. T. 2008. "Dual-Processing Accounts of Reasoning, Judgment, and Social Cognition." *Annual Review of Psychology* 59: 255–78.

Evers, Kathinka. 2010. *Neuroética.* Buenos Aires: Katz.

———. 2015. "Can We Be Epigenetically Proactive?" In *Open Mind*: 13 (T), edited by T. Metzinger and J. M. Windt, 1–21. Frankfurt am Main: MIND Group.

Fehr, Ernst, and Frédéric Schneider. 2010. "Eyes Are on Us, but Nobody Cares: Are Eye Cues Relevant for Strong Reciprocity?" *Proceedings of the Royal Society* 277: 1315–23.

Fleischacker, Samuel. 2004. *A Short History of Distributive Justice.* Cambridge, MA: Harvard University Press.

Fougeret de Montbron, Louis-Charles. 1970. *Le cosmopolite, ou Le citoyen du monde, suivi de la capitale des Gaules ou la nouvelle Babylone*. Edited by R. Trousson. Bordeaux: Ducros.

Francis, Pope Francis. 2015. *Laudato Si': Encyclical Letter on Care for Our Common Home*. https://www.vatican.va/content/francesco/en/encyclicals/documents/papa -francesco_20150524_enciclica-laudato-si.html.

Fuentes, Carlos. 2013. *Good Conscience: A Novel*. Translated by Sam Hilliman. New York: FSG.

Fuster, Joaquín M. 2014. *Cerebro y libertad*. Barcelona: Ariel.

García Delgado, José Luis, Ángela Triguero, and Juan Carlos Jiménez. 2014. "El emprendedor social como punto de encuentro entre el tercer sector y la sociedad civil." *Mediterráneo Económico* 26: 275–90.

García Márquez, Gabriel. 1970. *One Hundred Years of Solitude*. Translated by Gregory Rabassa. New York: Harper and Row.

García-Marzá, Domingo. 2004. *Ética empresarial. Del diálogo a la confianza*. Madrid: Trotta.

———. 2009. "¿Agentes de justicia? La responsabilidad social de las empresas como factor de desarrollo." In *Pobreza y libertad. Erradicar la pobreza desde el enfoque de las capacidades de Amartya Sen*, edited by Adela Cortina and Gustavo Pereira, 193–209. Madrid: Tecnos.

———. 2012. "Neuropolítica: una mirada crítica sobre el poder." In *Guía Comares de Neurofilosofía práctica*, edited by Adela Cortina, 77–96. Granada: Comares.

García Roca, Joaquín. 1998. *Exclusión social and contracultura de la solidaridad*. Madrid: Ediciones HOAC.

———. 2016. *Cristianismo. Nuevos horizontes, viejas fronteras*. Valencia: Diálogo.

Gazzaniga, Michael S. 2009. *The Ethical Brain*. New York: Dana Press.

Gintis, H. 2003. "The Hitchhiker's Guide to Altruism: Gene-Culture Coevolution and the Internalization of Norms." *Journal of Theoretical Biology* 220: 407–18.

Glucksmann, André. 2005. *El discurso del odio*. Madrid: Taurus.

Gómez, Carlos. 1998. "Conciencia." In *Diez palabras clave en ética*, edited by Adela Cortina, 17–71. Estella: Verbo Divino.

Gómez-Bezares, Fernando. 2001. *Ética, economía and finanzas*. La Rioja: Gobierno de La Rioja.

Goulet, Denis. 2006. *Development Ethics at Work: Explorations—1960–2002*. New York: Routledge.

Gracia, Diego. 1989. *Fundamentos de Bioética*. Madrid: EUDEMA.

Greene, Joshua D. 2012. "Del 'es' neuronal al 'debe' moral: ¿cuáles son las implicaciones morales de la psicología moral neurocientífica?" In *Guía Comares de Neurofilosofía práctica*, edited by Adela Cortina, 149–58. Granada: Comares.

Greene, Joshua D. 2014. "Beyond Point-and-Shoot Morality: Why Cognitive (Neuro) Science Matters for Ethics." *Ethics* 124: 695–726.

Habermas, Jürgen. 1990. *Moral Consciousness and Communicative Action.* Cambridge, MA: MIT Press.

———. 1991. "Justicia and solidaridad." In *Ética comunicativa y democracia,* edited by K. O. Apel, A. Cortina, J. De Zan, and D. Michelini, 175–205. Barcelona: Crítica.

———. 1994. "On the Pragmatic, the Ethical, and the Moral Employments of Practical Reason." In *Justificatiion and Application: Remarks on Discourse Ethics,* translated by Ciaran Cronin, 1–18. Cambridge, MA: MIT Press.

———. 1998. *The Inclusion of the Other: Studies in Political Theory.* London: Polity Press, 1998.

———. 2003. *The Future of Human Nature.* London: Polity.

———. 2015. "Kant's Idea of Perpetual Peace: At 200 Years' Remove." In *The Inclusion of the Other.* London: Polity.

———. 2018. *Philosophical-Political Profiles.* London: Polity.

Haidt, Jonathan. 2012a. "El perro emocional y su cola racional." In *Guía Comares de Neurofilosofía práctica,* edited by Adela Cortina, 159–215. Granada: Comares.

———. 2012b. *The Righteous Mind: Why Good People Are Divided by Politics and Religion.* New York: Pantheon Books.

Hamilton, W. D. 1964a. "The Evolution of Altruistic Behavior." *American Naturalist* (97): 354–56.

———. 1964b. "The Genetical Evolution of Social Behavior." *Journal of Theoretical Biology* (7): 1–52.

Hare, Ivan, and James Weinstein, eds. 2010. *Extreme Speech and Democracy.* New York: Oxford University Press.

Harris, John. 2009. "Enhancements Are a Moral Obligation." In *Human Enhancement,* edited by Julian Savulescu and Nick Bostrom, 131–54. Oxford: Oxford University Press.

———. 2016. *How to Be Good. The Possibility of Moral Enhancement.* New York: Oxford University Press.

Hauser, Marc. 2009. *Moral Minds: The Nature of Right and Wrong.* New York: HarperCollins.

Hegel, Georg Wilhelm Friedrich. 2001. *Philosophy of Right.* Translated by S. W. Dyde. Kitchener, ON: Batoche Books.

Hill, Thomas E., Jr. 2002. "Four Conceptions of Conscience." In *Integrity and Conscience,* edited by Ian Shapiro and Robert Adams, 13–52. New York: New York University Press.

Hirschman, Albert O. 2013. *The Passions and the Interests: Political Arguments for Capitalism before Its Triumph.* Princeton, NJ: Princeton University Press.

Hobbes, Thomas. 1651. *Leviathan.*

Honneth, Axel. 1996. *The Struggle for Recognition: the Moral Grammar of Social Conflicts*. Cambridge, MA: MIT Press.

Hughes, James. 2004. *Citizen Cyborg: Why Democratic Societies Must Respond to the Redesigned Human of the Future*. Boulder, CO: Westview Press.

Hume, David. 1739. *A Treatise of Human Nature*.

Iacoboni, Marco. 2008. *Mirroring People: The New Science of How We Connect with Others*. New York: FSG.

Iglesias, Enrique. 2008. "Estrategia para erradicar la pobreza in el siglo xxi." In *La ética en la estrategia empresarial del siglo xxi*, 137–50. Valencia: Fundación ÉTNOR.

Ito, A., T. Fujii, A. Ueno, Y. Koseki, M. Tashiro, and E. Mori. 2010–2011. "Neural Basis of Pleasant and Unpleasant Emotions Induced by Social Reputation." *CYRIC Annual Report*, 100–102, Tohoku University, Sendai, Japan.

Izuma, Keise. 2012. "The Social Neuroscience of Reputation." *Neuroscience Research* 72: 283–88.

Jacobs, James B., and Kimberly Potter. 1998. *Hate Crimes: Criminal Law and Identity Politics*. New York: Oxford University Press.

Jensen, K., J. Call, and M. Tomasello. 2007. "Chimpanzees Are Rational Maximizers in an Ultimate Game." *Science* 318 (5847): 107–9.

Jonas, Hans. 1984. *The Imperative of Responsibility*. Chicago: University of Chicago Press.

Joyce, Richard. 2014. "The Origins of Moral Judgement." In *Evolved Morality: The Biology and Philosophy of Human Conscience*, edited by Frans B. M. de Waal, Patricia S. Churchland, Telmo Pievanim, and Stefano Parmigiani, 261–78. Leiden: Brill.

Kahneman, Daniel. 2011. *Thinking, Fast and Slow*. London: Penguin Books.

Kant, Immanuel. 1991. *The Metaphysics of Morals*. Translated by Mary Gregor. Cambridge: Cambridge University Press.

———. 1997. *Lectures on Ethics*. Translated by Peter Heath. Cambridge: Cambridge University Press.

———. 2006. *Toward Perpetual Peace and Other Writings on Politics, Peace, and History*. Translated by David Colclasure. New Haven, CT: Yale University Press.

———. 2007. *Anthropology, History, and Education*. Translated by Robert B. Loudon and Günther Zöller. New York: Cambridge University Press.

———. 2012. *Groundwork for the Metaphysics of Morals*. Translated by Mary Gregor and Jens Timmerman. Cambridge: Cambridge University Press.

Kohlberg, Lawrence. 1981. *The Philosophy of Moral Development*. New York: Harper.

Krause, Sharon R. 2008. *Civil Passions. Moral Sentiment and Democratic Deliberation*. Princeton, NJ: Princeton University Press.

Lamo de Espinosa, Emilio. 2014. "La globalización cultural: ¿crisol, ensalada o gazpacho?" *Mediterráneo Económico* (26): 389–407.

Lévinas, Emmanuel. 1965. *Totality and Infinity: An Essay on Exteriority.* Translated by Alphonso Lingis. Pittsburgh: Duquesne University Press.

———. 1995. *Ethics and Infinity: Conversations with Philippe Nemo.* Translated and with an introduction by Richard A. Cohen. Ann Arbor, MI: XanEdu.

Levy, Neil. 2007. *Neuroethics.* New York: Cambridge University Press.

Lewontin, Richard, Steven Rose, and Leon J. Kamin. 2017. *Not in Our Genes: Biology, Ideology, and Human Nature.* Chicago: Haymarket Books.

Liao, S. Matthew, ed. 2016. *Moral Brains. The Neuroscience of Morality.* New York: Oxford University Press.

Loewenstein, Karl. 1937a. "Militant Democracy and Fundamental Rights." *American Political Science Review* 31 (3): 417–32.

———. 1937b. "Militant Democracy and Fundamental Rights." *American Political Science Review* 31 (4): 638–58.

Lozano, José Félix. 2004. *Códigos éticos para el mundo empresarial.* Madrid: Trotta.

Marcus, George E. 2002. *The Sentimental Citizen: Emotion in Democratic Politics.* Harrisburg: Pennsylvania State University Press.

Marshall, T. H., and Tom Bottomore. 1987. *Citizenship and Social Class.* London: Pluto Press.

Martínez Navarro, Emilio. 2000. *Ética para el desarrollo de los pueblos.* Madrid: Trotta.

———. 2002. "Aporofobia." In *Glosario para una sociedad intercultural,* edited by Jesús Conill, 17–23. Valencia: Bancaja.

Martínez-Torrón, Javier. 2016. "Libertad de expresión y lenguaje ofensivo: algunos criterios prácticos de análisis jurídico." *El Cronista del Estado social y democrático de derecho* (60): 26–33.

Milanovic, Branko. 2016. *Global Inequality. A New Approach for the Age of Globalization.* Cambridge, MA: The Belknap Press of Harvard University Press.

Milton, John. 1611. *Aeropagitica.*

Ministerio del Interior. 2015. *Informe sobre incidentes relacionados con los delitos de odio in España, 2014.* Madrid.

Ministerio del Interior. 2016. *Informe sobre la evolución de los delitos de odio en España, 2015.* Madrid.

Minsky, Marvin. 1985. *Society of Mind.* New York: Simon and Schuster.

Moll, Jorge, Ricardo de Oliveira-Souza, Paul J. Eslinger, et al. 2002. "The Neural Correlates of Moral Sensitivity: A Functional Magnetic Resonance Imaging Investigation of Basic and Moral Emotions." *Journal of Neuroscience* 22 (7): 2730–36.

———. 2005. "The Neural Basis of Human Moral Cognition." *Nature Reviews Neuroscience* (6): 799–809.

Morell, Antonio. 2002. *La legitimación social de la pobreza.* Barcelona: Anthropos.

Moreno, José Ángel. 2014. "Semillas de economía alternative." In *La responsabilidad ética de la sociedad civil, Mediterráneo Económico*, vol. 26, edited by Adela Cortina, 291–307. Cajamar: Madrid.

Moretón Toquero, M.a Aránzazu. 2012. "El 'ciberodio', la nueva cara del mensaje de odio: entre la cibercriminalidad y la libertad de expresión." *Revista Jurídica de Castilla y León* (27): 1–18.

Morgado, Ignacio. 2010. *Emociones e inteligencia social.* Barcelona: Ariel.

Mori, Massimo. 2006. "Kant and Cosmopolitanism." In *Immanuel Kant nos 200 anos da sua morte,* edited by Manuel Cândido Pimentel, Carlos Morujâo, and Miguel Santos Silva, 307–20. Lisboa: Universidade Catolica Editora.

Muñoz Machado, Santiago. 2013. *Los itinerarios de la libertad de palabra.* Madrid: Real Academia Española.

Nietzsche, Friedrich. 1999. *Die fröhliche Wissenschaft.* Edited by Giorgio Colli and Mazzino Montinari. Vol. 3 of *Kritische Studien Ausgabe.* Berlin: De Gruyter.

Novales, Alfonso. 2011. "Crecimiento económico, desigualdad y pobreza." Lecture at the Royal Academy of Moral and Political Sciences, June 21, 2011.

———. 2015. "Austeridad and desigualdad." Lecture at the Royal Academy of Moral and Political Sciences, February 24, 2015.

Nowak, Martin A., Karen M. Page, and Karl Sigmund. 2000. "Fairness versus Reason in the Ultimatum Game." *Science* 289 (5485): 1773–75.

Nowak, Martin A., and Karl Sigmund. 2000. "Shrewd Investments." *Science* 288, (5467): 819–20.

Nuccetelli, Susana, and Gary Shea, eds. 2012. *Ethical Naturalism: Current Debates.* Cambridge: Cambridge University Press.

Observatorio Hatento. 2015a. *Muchas preguntas. Algunas respuestas. Los delitos de odio contra las personas sin hoga.* Madrid: RAIS Fundación. https://www.hatento.org.

———. 2015b. *Informe de investigación.* Madrid: RAIS Fundación.

Ojakangas, Mika. 2013. *The Voice of Conscience. A Political Genealogy of Western Ethical Experience.* New York: Bloomsbury.

Olinto P., G. Lara, and J. Saavedra. 2014. "Accelerating Poverty Reduction in a Less Poor World: The Roles of Growth and Inequality." *Policy Research Working Paper 6855.* Washington, DC: The World Bank, Poverty Reduction and Equity Unit.

Ortega, César. 2016. "¿Naturalizar la idea de justicia? Una respuesta crítica desde la teoría moral de Jürgen Habermas." *Pensamiento* (272): in press.

Parekh, Bikuh. 2002. *Rethinking Multiculturalism: Cultural Diversity and Political Theory.* Cambridge, MA: Harvard University Press.

———. 2006. "Hate Speech: Is There a Case for Banning?" *Public Policy Research* 12 (4): 213ff.

Pedrajas, Marta, and Samuel Choritz. 2016. *Getting to the Last Mile in Least Developed Countries*. New York: United Nations Development Program.

Pereira, Gustavo. 2013. *Elements of a Critical Theory of Justice*. London: Palgrave Macmillan.

Piketty, Thomas. 2017. *Capital in the Twentieth Century*. Translated by Arthur Goldhammer. Cambridge, MA: Harvard University Press.

Pinilla, Rafael. 2004. *La renta básica de ciudadanía*. Barcelona: Icaria.

———. 2006. *Más allá del bienestar. La renta básica de la ciudadanía como innovación social basada en la evidencia*. Barcelona: Icaria.

Pires, María do Céu. 2015. *Ética e cidadanía. Um Diálogo com Adela Cortina*. Lisbon: Colibrí.

Plato. *Collected Dialogues*, edited by Edith Hamilton and Huntington Cairns. Princeton, NJ: Princeton University Press, 1961.

Pogge, Thomas. 2008. *World Poverty and Human Rights*. London: Polity.

Post, Robert. 2009. "Hate Speech." In *Extreme Speech and Democracy*, edited by Ivan Hare and James Weinstein, 129–38. New York: Oxford University Press.

Ravallion, Martin. 2016. *The Economics of Poverty. History, Measurement, and Policy*. Oxford: Oxford University Press.

Raventós, Daniel. 1999. *El derecho a la existencia*. Barcelona: Ariel.

———. 2001. *La renta básica. Por una ciudadanía más libre, más igualitaria y más fraternal*. Barcelona: Ariel.

Rawls, John. 1971. *A Theory of Justice*. Oxford: Oxford University Press.

Rawls, John. 2005. *Political Liberalism*. New York: Cambridge University Press.

Renaut, Alain. 1999. *The Era of the Individual: Contribution to a Theory of Subjectivity*. Translated by M. B. DeBevoise and Franklin Philip. Delhi: Motilal Banarsidass.

Renaut, Alain, and Patrick Savidan. 1999. "Les lumières critiques: Rousseau, Kant et Fichte." In *Histoire de la philosophie politique*, vol. 3, edited by Alain Renaut. Paris: Calmann-Lévy.

"Retos actuales de la neuroética. Current Challenges for Neuroethics." 2013. *Recerca. Revista de Pensament i Anàlisi* (13):1–207.

Revenga, Miguel, ed. 2015a. *Libertad de expresión y discursos del odio*. Madrid: Cátedra de Democracia y Derechos Humanos.

———. 2015b. "Los discursos del odio y la democracia adjetivada: tolerante, intransigente, ¿militante?" In *Libertad de expresión and discursos del odio*, edited by Miguel Revenga, 15–32. Madrid: Cátedra de Democracia and Derechos Humanos, Universidad de Alcalá and Defensor del Pueblo.

Rey, Fernando. 2015. "Discurso del odio y racismo líquido." In Miguel Revenga (dir.), *Libertad de expresión y discursos del odio*, 51–88. Madrid: Cátedra de Democracia and Derechos Humanos.

Richart, Andrés. 2016. "El origen evolutivo de la agencia moral y sus implicaciones para la ética." *Pensamiento* 72 (273): 849–64.

Ricœur, Paul. 2005. *The Course of Recognition.* Translated by David Pellauer. Cambridge, MA: Harvard University Press.

Rizzolatti, Giacomo, and Corrado Sinigaglia. 2006. *Las neuronas espejo.* Barcelona: Paidós.

Rodríguez-Izquierdo, Myriam. 2015. "El discurso del odio a través de internet." In *Libertad de expresión y discursos del odio,* edited by Miguel Revenga, 149–83. Madrid: Cátedra de Democracia and Derechos Humanos.

Rousseau, Jean-Jacques. 1979. *Émile, or On Education.* Translated by Allan Bloom. New York: Basic Books.

Ruggie, John Gerard. 2013. *Just Business. Multinational Corporations and Human Rights.* New York: W. W. Norton & Company.

Safire, William. 2002. "Visions for a New Field of 'Neuroethics.'" In *Neuroethics: Mapping the Field,* edited by S. J. Marcus, 3–9. New York: The Dana Press.

Sachs, Jeffrey. 2005. *The End of Poverty. Economic Possibilities for Our Time.* New York: Penguin.

———. 2015. *The Age of Sustainable Development.* New York: Cambridge University Press.

Sánchez Meca, Diego. 2006. "Com-padecer/sim-patizar: Hacia una filosofía de la hospitalidad." In *Filosofía y dolor,* edited by Moisés González, 471–89. Madrid: Tecnos.

Sandel, Michael. 2007. *The Case against Perfection.* Cambridge, MA: Harvard University Press.

Savulescu, Julian. 2012. *¿Decisiones peligrosas? Una bioética desafiante.* Madrid: Tecnos.

Savulescu, Julian, and Nick Bostrom, eds. 2009. *Human Enhancement.* Oxford: Oxford University Press.

Schwartz, Pedro. 2016. "La desigualdad: falso problema." Lecture at the Royal Academy of Moral and Political Sciences, February 9, 2016.

Searle, John. 1970. *Speech Acts.* Cambridge: Cambridge University Press.

Secretaría de Estado de Seguridad del Ministerio del Interior. 2014. *Informe sobre la evolución de los delitos de odio en España, 2013.* Madrid: Ministerio del Interior.

———. 2015. *Informe sobre incidentes relacionados con los delitos de odio en España, 2014.* Madrid: Ministerio del Interior.

Seinen, I., and A. Schram. 2006. "Social Status and Group Norms: Indirect Reciprocity in a Repeated Helping Experiment." *European Economic Review.* 50: 581–602.

Sen, Amartya. 1977. "Rational Fools: A Critique of the Behavioural Foundations of Economic Theory." *Philosophy and Public Affairs* 6 (4): 317–44.

Sen, Amartya. 1985. *Commodities and Capabilities*. Amsterdam: North-Holland.

———. 2001. *Development as Freedom*. New York: Oxford University Press.

———. 2002. *Rationality and Freedom*. Cambridge, MA: The Belknap Press of Harvard University Press.

———. 2004. "Elements of a Theory of Human Rights." *Philosophy and Public Affairs* 32 (4): 315–56.

Seneca. 2015. *Letters on Ethics: To Lucilius*. Translated by Margaret Graver. Chicago: University of Chicago Press.

Simon, Herbert. 1990. "A Mechanism for Social Selection and Successful Altruism." *Science* 250: 1665–68.

Siurana, Juan Carlos. 2003. *Una brújula para la vida moral*. Granada: Comares.

Skyrms, Brian. 1996. *Evolution of the Social Contract*. Cambridge: Cambridge University Press.

Smith, Adam. 1759. *The Theory of Moral Sentiments*.

———. 1776. *An Inquiry into the Nature and Causes of the Wealth of Nations*.

Streeten, Paul, Shahid Javed Burki, World Bank, et al. 1981. *First Things First. Meeting Basic Human Needs in Developing Countries*. Oxford: Oxford University Press.

Suhler, Christopher, and Patricia Churchland. 2011. "The Neurological Basis of Morality." In *The Oxford Handbook of Neuroethics*, edited by Judy Illes and Barbara J. Sahakian, 33–58. New York: Oxford University Press.

Terceiro, Jaime. 2016. "Desigualdad and economía clientelar." Lecture at the Royal Academy of Moral and Political Sciences, June 21, 2016.

Tomasello, Michael. 2009. *Why We Cooperate*. 2009. Cambridge, MA: MIT Press.

Torralba, Francesc. 2004. *"No olvidéis la hospitalidad." Una exploración teológica*. Madrid: PPC.

———. 2005. *Sobre la hospitalidad*. Madrid: PPC.

Tortosa, José M. 2002. "Pobreza." In *Glosario para una sociedad intercultural*, edited by Jesús Conill, 281–88. Valencia: Bancaja.

Trivers, R. L. 1971. "The Evolution of Reciprocal Altruism." *Quarterly Review of Biology* 46: 35–57.

Van Parijs, Philippe. 1995. *Real Freedom for All*. New York: Oxford University Press.

Velarde, Juan. 2014. "Ética de las finanzas." *Mediterráneo Económico* 26: 191–207.

Vives, Antonio. 2010. *La responsabilidad social de las empresas: enfoques ante la crisis*. Madrid: Fundación Carolina.

Vives, Juan Luis. 2006. *Tratado del socorro de los pobres*. Valencia: Pre-textos.

Vlachos, Georges. 1962. *La pensée politique de Kant. Métaphysique de l'ordre et dialectique du progrès*. Paris: Presses Universitaires de France.

Waal, Frans M. de, Patricia S. Churchland, Telmo Pievani, and Stefano Parmigiani, eds. 2014. *Evolved Morality. The Biology and Philosophy of Human Conscience*. Boston: Brill.

Walker, Samuel, 1994. *Hate Speech. The History of an American Controversy.* Lincoln: University of Nebraska Press.

Wedekind, C., and M. Milinski. 2000. "Cooperation through Image Scoring in Humans." *Science* 288: 850–52.

Wilson, J. Q. 1993. *The Moral Sense.* New York: Free Press.

Wiseman, Harris. 2016. *The Myth of the Moral Brain: The Limits of Moral Enhancement.* Cambridge, MA: MIT Press.

Zamagni, Stefano. 2014. "El reto de la responsabilidad civil de la empresa." *Mediterráneo Económico* 26: 209–25.

Zweig, Stefan. 1953. *Beware of Pity.* Translated by Phyllis and Trevor Blewitt. London: Cassell.

Index

ABC Cultural, 6
Abraham, 130–31
Access Age, 119
accountability, 82
action: altruism and, 60–62; aversion
 and, 57; communitarianism and, 46,
 48, 58, 64; compassion and, 62, 65;
 conflict and, 54, 56, 58, 62, 64;
 contempt and, 45; contractualism
 and, 63–64, 94; cooperation and,
 58, 62–65; declarations and, 47–50,
 57; democracy and, 45–46, 49;
 dignity and, 47, 50, 66; discrimination and, 49, 58; duty and, 46 (see
 also duty); education and, 48, 64;
 ethics and, 46, 48–49, 56–60; ethnic
 groups and, 44, 48; exclusion and,
 47, 60–65; fear and, 45, 52, 56;
 honor and, 64; ideals and, 45, 51;
 ideology and, 52, 58, 63; immigrants
 and, 46; inequality and, 49; justice
 and, 46–48; Kant and, 50, 63; legal
 issues and, 55; liberalism and, 45,
 47; love and, 50, 61; morals and,
 46–50, 53, 58–64; neuroscience and,
 51–53; norms and, 48, 63; philosophy and, 50; politics and, 46–47;
 poverty and, 6–7, 46, 49; race and,
 47–48, 50, 57, 59, 63–64; radicalism

and, 50–51, 64; rationality and, 54,
 62–63; reciprocity and, 62–63, 71–72,
 76, 94–95, 125–26; refugees and, 46;
 rejection and, 57; respect and, 11, 37,
 39, 43–44; selfishness and, 48, 50,
 60, 62–63, 65; tradition and, 65;
 values and, 45, 48, 53, 58–59; virtues
 and, 54; war and, 60–61; wealth
 and, 46; xenophobia and, 45, 47,
 51, 55–56, 59–61, 64
Adam and Eve, 50, 73
Afghanistan, xix, 127
Africa, xi, 72, 128
Agar, 89
Age of Sustainable Development, 119
aggression: external, 15; hate crimes
 and, 15, 18, 25–26; morals and,
 72–73, 91, 97, 99–100
Albania, xix
Alcaeus of Mytilene, 55
Almeria, 20
altruism: action and, 60–62;
 conscience and, 71–73, 76; moral
 bioenhancement and, 93–95
Amatrice earthquake, 30
Amri, Anis, 22
Andrews, Lori, 89
Annan, Kofi, 123
Annas, George, 89–90

104–26; Kant and, 127–41, 144; Ortega on, 129; radical individualism and, 134; Spain and, 128; United Nations and, x, 129, 143; Universal Declaration of Human Rights and, x, 129

cosmopolite, ou Le citoyen du monde, Le (Fougeret de Montbron), 134

courtesy, 132

COVID-19 pandemic, x–xi

Critique of Judgment (Kant), 137

Crocker, David, xiv, 119

Cuenca, 20

cyberethics, 39

cyberspace, 30–31

Cynics, 110

Damasio, Antonio, 51

Darwin, Charles: altruism and, 60; group selection and, 61, 93–94; morals and, 61, 70–72, 79–80

Dawkins, Richard, 62, 94

debtors' prisons, 103

Decade of the Brain, 52

declarations: action and, 47–50, 57; inequality and, 109, 117; moral bioenhancement and, 84, 88; Universal Declaration of Human Rights, x, 47–49, 117, 129

DeGrazia, 89

democracy: action and, 45–46, 49; Barber on, 36; citizens and, 36–37, 82; dignity and, 8, 44; economic issues and, xiii–xiv; hate speech and, 30–31, 34–39, 42, 44; inclusive, 46; inequality and, 105, 115; Loewenstein on, 35; militant, 34–38; moral bioenhancement and, 88, 101; participatory, 36;

radical, 34–39; Revenga on, 34–35; strong, 36; unitary, 36–37; xenophobia and, 2

deontology, 117–19

Derrida, Jacques, 140–41

Descartes's Error (Damasio), 51

De Waal, Frans B. M., 71

Dictionary of the Spanish Language, 9

Digital Age, 119

dignity: action and, 47, 50, 66; asylum and, ix; aversion and, 6–7; compassion and, 11–12; conscience and, 66, 81, 83; democracy and, 8, 44; discrimination and, 8–9, 11–12; duty and, 10; empowerment and, 10; equal, 9–12, 26, 50, 66, 106; esteem and, 21, 32, 34, 37, 43–44, 75, 81–82, 114, 118, 132; ethics and, 12, 23, 39, 44, 126, 144; fear and, 7–10; hate crimes and, 13, 23, 26–27; hate speech and, 13, 23, 26–27, 32, 39, 43–44; homeless and, 9–10; honor and, 125 (*see also* honor); hospitality and, 139, 144–45; hostility and, 9; immigrants and, 10; inequality and, 106, 112, 117–18, 120, 125–26; Kant and, 11; liberty and, 120; moral bioenhancement and, 85; peace and, 12, 32, 120; politics and, 6–7; race and, 7–9; reciprocity and, 104; refugees and, 6; rejection and, 6–10; respect and, xii, xxi, 83, 88, 123, 141; Universal Declaration of Human Rights and, x, 47–49, 117, 129; violation of, 4; xenophobia and, 3–4, 7–8

disabled people, 8–9, 90

Discourse of Hate, The (Glucksmann), 14–15, 18

Jesus, 79, 113

Jews: antisemitism and, xii, 14–15, 55; charity and, 116; Gibson diatribe against, 55; hate crimes and, 21; hate speech and, 35; Holocaust denial and, 35; inequality and, 116; original sin and, 50; Skokie case and, 35

jihadist attacks, 128

jobs, 22, 64, 125

Jonas, Hans, 69, 93

Journal of Evolution and Technology, 88

Journal of Transhumanism, 88

judges, 25–26, 40

justice: action and, 46–48; burdens of, 33; compassion and, 143–45; conscience and, 68, 75, 78, 83; hate crimes and, 14, 18, 22–23, 27; hate speech and, 33, 44; hospitality and, 143–45; inequality and, 106–7, 109, 111, 115–26; minimum of, 22–23; moral bioenhancement and, 84–85, 90, 94; nature of, 44; pluralism and, 22, 44, 46; sense of, 14, 18, 47, 120

Kant, Immanuel, xiv; action and, 50, 63; categorization and, 23, 129; conscience and, 80–82, 152n33; cosmopolitan society and, 127–41, 144; *Critique of Judgment*, 137; deontological tradition of, 117–19; dignity and, 11; Doctrine of Right and, 133, 136, 138; on education, 127; embedded individual and, 133; ethics and, 132, 156n16; Formula of the End in Itself and, 112; on freedom, 37–38; hate crimes and, 23; hate speech and, 37–38; hospitality and, 127–41, 144, 156nn16–17; *humanitas aesthetica* of, 132; inequality and, 112, 117–18;

Lectures on Ethics, 132, 136; *The Metaphysics of Morals*, 80, 82, 132–33, 136, 138; moral bioenhancement and, 86, 96, 102–3; on obligation, 38, 80–82, 129, 133; *Pedagogy*, 127; *Perpetual Peace*, 63, 133–36; on social virtues, 131–33

Kass, Leon, 89

King, Martin Luther, 45

Kohlberg, Lawrence, 47–48

Krause, Sharon R., 96

Kropotkin, Peter, 63

Lady Liberty, x

Land of Nod, 73

La Vanguardia newspaper, 20

Lebanon, xix

Lectures on Ethics (Kant), 132, 136

legal issues: action and, 55; burdens of justice, 33; citizens and, 38, 134; conscience and, 73, 79, 81; constitutions, 31–37, 49, 82, 109, 136–39; First Amendment, 35; freedom of expression, 3, 31–39, 43–44; hate crimes, 2, 16, 23–27; hate speech, 30–39, 44; hospitality and, 133–42, 145; inequality and, 117, 122; morals and, 85, 89, 94; rule of law, xxi, 117; U.S. Supreme Court, 35

Lessing, Gotthold Ephraim, 134

Lévinas, Emmanuel, 69, 140–41, 143

liberalism: action and, 45, 47; hate speech and, 32, 36; hospitality and, 140; inequality and, 119; moral bioenhancement and, 88, 96, 101; tradition and, xii

liberty: dignity and, 120; hate speech and, 35, 38–39, 42, 44–45; peace and, 120

morals (*continued*)

citizens and, 37, 44, 48–49, 82, 88, 95–96, 102, 136; conscience and, 66–82; corruption and, 69, 74, 81, 84, 104–5, 121–22; Darwin and, 61, 71–72, 79–80; De Waal on, 71; duty and, 8, 50, 80, 103, 106, 133, 135; economic issues and, 88, 92, 94, 102; education and, 28, 69, 84–85, 96–103; ethics and, 7–8 (*see also* ethics); evolution and, 39, 48, 70–74, 78–79, 88, 93, 95, 98–99; freedom and, 37–38; guilt and, 25–26, 73, 81, 97; Haidt and, 69–70; hate crimes and, 17, 21–22, 28; hate speech and, 37–40, 44; hospitality and, 128, 132–40, 144; inequality and, 104–6, 109, 115, 121–22; Kant on, 80, 82; Kohlberg on, 47–48; legal issues and, 85, 89, 94; Moll on, 69; norms and, 80 (*see also* norms); obligation and, 38, 69, 78, 80–82, 106, 132–33, 135, 140; obligation to help poor, 106–7; politics and, 7, 9, 39, 47, 84–85, 96; poverty and, 104–6, 109, 115, 121–22; selfishness and, 48, 50, 62, 69–70, 74, 80–81, 93–94; shame and, 13, 64, 72–76, 97; thought morality, 49; Trivers and, 72; values and, 70 (*see also* values); written morality, 49

More, Thomas, 149n13

Moreno, José Ángel, 124

Mori, Massimo, 134

Mounier, Emmanuel, 67, 77

Muñoz Machado, Santiago, 115, 149n13

Münzer, Thomas, 116

Muslims, xxi, 2; *Charlie Hebdo* massacre and, 30; hate crimes and, 17–20, 22; jihadist attacks and, 128; Mohammad, 30; sharing and, 116

Mutual Aid: A Factor of Evolution (Kropotkin), 63

myths, 21, 130

National Front, 129

nationalism, xx, 128

Native Americans, xi

Nazis, 35–36

nepotism, 64

Netherlands, xx

Neuroeducation in Cordial Virtues (Codina), 85

neuroethics, 58–60, 86–87, 98

neuroscience, 51–53, 91–92, 94

New Bottles of New Wine (Huxley), 88

New Testament, 116, 131

Nicaraguans, ix

Nietzsche, Friedrich, 66–67, 77, 87–88

Nigeria, xix

Nobodies, The (Galeano), 8

norms: action and, 48, 63; communitarianism and, 48, 72, 78; conscience and, 70–74, 78–81; ideals and, 8; moral bioenhancement and, 84, 94–95

North Korea, 33

Novales, Alfonso, 121

Nowak, Martin A., 75–76

Nuremberg Code, 100

Nussbaum, Martha, xiv, 28, 119

Obama, Barack, 52

obligation: conscience and, 69, 76, 78, 80–83; hospitality and, 129–35, 140; inequality and, 106–7, 117, 124; internal, 81; Kant on, 38, 80–82, 129,